Keith Shackleton —

If the Earth had been formed a year ago, on January 1st, life would have arrived on December 10th, only to vanish some sixteen days later.

Man, *Homo sapiens*, would only have showed up very late on December 31st, in fact at around ten minutes to midnight.

A few minutes later, and *in less than one minute*, man has drastically altered the fragile balance between the land, the seas and the atmosphere.

In January 2006, NASA climatologist James Hansen again defied United States federal attempts to gag him.

He told reporters about the sustainability of Greenland's ice shelf saying: "We can't let it go on for another ten years like this." If we did? Over time, the build-up of CO_2 emissions would, he concluded, "imply changes that constitute practically a different planet with less than ten years to reverse course.

So, not in our children's lifetimes, nor in our grandchildren's, but in ours!"

James E Hansen heads NASA's Goddard Institute for space studies and is also visiting professor at Columbia University's Earth and Environmental Sciences Division. Best known for his testimonies on climate change to the congressional committees during the '80s, he helped raise the initial broad awareness of global warming. He is a key promoter of new technologies as a means of reducing planet damage; he continues to be an outspoken critic of past and the present Bush administration's indifference to the environment.

Greenland White-fronted Goose
Anser albifrons flavirostris

face to face
with nature

with my best wishes,

david chaffe

First published in 2007 by
Stormforce Publications,
Little Weare Cottage, Weare Giffard, North Devon, EX39 4QZ
+44 (0)1237 425019
website: www.stormforcepublications.co.uk
e-mail: books@stormforcepublications.co.uk

© David Chaffe 2007

isbn: 978-0-9534676-9-3

Printed and bound by
R Booth Ltd
Mabe, Penryn, Cornwall, TR10 9HH

Paper from
Sustainable forests

for Peter Scott
　... who, although he didn't know, first enticed me to remote wetland places and so to the wild creatures that live there ... quite simply, he guided me into the path of my life's work and passion.

but especially for Olivia, our daughter
　... Helen and I hope that one of Olivia's gifts to life will be to further the conservation of our greatest treasure, the environment of planet Earth, by making her own inimitable and enduring mark.

"... those who contemplate the beauty of the earth will find reserves of strength that will last as long as life lasts ..."

Rachel Carson (1907-1964)
US Marine Biologist and author of *Silent Spring,* 1962

Contents

BARNACLE GOOSE

This lovely family group came closer & closer as I watched

one of the adults is always alert.

High in the far north - even before the last snows have melted away the Barnacle's have young. The adult birds tend the young closely.

OTTER (Dog)

As I was looking over the river valley I became suddenly aware of being watched - An old dog otter had silently appeared among the waterside plants - I got to know this animal well

Barn Owls are magical birds - appearing from nowhere at dusk & then vanishing.

BARN OWL

I watched this Barn Owl quarter the rough grass meadow - at times he comes very close, oblivious to me

Foreword

"ONCE UPON A TIME ... WHEN THE WORLD WAS MINE"

I thought it would last my time
The sense that, beyond the town,
There would always be fields and farms ...

Earth will always respond
However we mess it about
Chuck filth in the sea, if you must
The tides will be clean beyond,

It seems just now
To be happening so very fast
For the first time I feel somehow
That it isn't going to last.

from "Going Going", Philip Larkin 1972
reproduced from *The Independent*, October 17th 2005

There are times in human history when all the world seems astir. A wind blows through human affairs which cannot be easily explained even by the most modern channels of communication. In popular words, we say that something is 'in the air'.

In 1848, Europe had felt the stirrings of revolution, from Karl Marx's writings in the British Museum in London to the turbulence of central Europe and the insights of Kierkegaard. Nearly a century later, at the end of the Second World War, and less than three decades after the Great War which was supposedly fought to end all wars, Winston Churchill was describing how an Iron Curtain had fallen over the same western and central Europe. Just twenty years later, Harold MacMillan was referring to phenomena and events in Africa as a 'wind of change'.

In June 1972, the nations of the world gathered in Stockholm to discuss, for the first time, the problems of world-wide pollution. As a young naturalist, a few years after reading for an honours degree in Geography at Pembroke College, Cambridge, I was hoping that history would now be taking a new turn as the United Kingdom, Europe and the world would subsequently live in the aftermath and results of the conference's words. Were we about to enter the dawn of a new age when the quality of life would become more important than the quantity of material gains squeezed out of life at every opportunity? If the recommendations of Stockholm were purposefully and honestly interpreted, then the stirrings would be detected from as far afield as Cornwall to China.

Alas, to no avail. Similar conferences at Rio and in Kyoto have followed Stockholm. A host of promises and platitudes by successive governments, both here at home and also abroad, have similarly indicated that man would not and will not be allowed to manipulate his environment. The reality is that our government, regardless of political leaning, has encouraged us to do exactly the opposite. Indeed, the ever-expanding European Union has permitted us, albeit by unequal subsidies, to 'impose ourselves upon wild nature'.

The considered conclusions of the conferences have come and gone. Deforestation, overgrazing, monoculture and the over-exploitation of square mile upon square mile of land and ocean, all continue to be detrimental moves on a large scale. Together with others of smaller but no less significant proportions, such as the grubbing up of hedgerows, and the repeated drenchings of the land with aritificial fertilisers, weed-killers and insecticides, mean that we have witnessed grievous and irreversible damage being done to the balance of the world natural.

Of course, as a lover of natural history still working to put my message across to young people, I am inclined to arrive at a pessimistic conclusion for the future of Planet Earth. I can still enjoy a few of the earth's incomparable true wildernesses where the flow of earth, atmosphere, plant and animal-life still remains untouched. They reflect the balance of nature in its true sense, having survived since time immemorial. In the United Kingdom and in Europe where there is more apparent and reported evidence, I see these areas being encroached upon year by year; I see the strongholds of the world natural falling one by one and despair at the thought of what seems, sadly, an inevitable process if our destiny is to be fulfilled. I see us hell-bent on seeking to turn the world natural ever more to our own advantage. As do many others, I conclude that we are also determined to create our own destruction as well. So I can reasonably conclude that, soon, there could be no room on this earth for both wild nature and ourselves.

So, have I any hope for the future then?

The truth is that the division of our world from the world of wild nature is a false and exceedingly dangerous division; false because it attempts to divide the things which are indivisible, that are indeed not two but one. It is dangerous because in trying to bring it about, we will render this earth uninhabitable as surely by its human as by its non-human occupants. The dawn of that new age of thought was beginning as my teenage and university years passed, before certain naturalists, other lovers of wild nature, led the new thought and change. They came of age and were of a similar understanding almost simultaneously. In the 1950s Peter Scott, Ronald Lockley and Gerald Durrell were quickly realising that, severe as other threats were, and still are, ecology was the science of the utmost importance. Another group, the field scientists at Monks Wood

The author with R M Lockley; Peter Scott, Ronald Lockley and Gerald Durrell, were already realising, during the 1950s, that ecology was the science of the utmost importance.

© Jim Hale, 1969; courtesy Mia Hale

Research Station in Cambridgeshire, among whom were Drs Ratcliffe (peregrine falcons), Jefferies (otters) and Bellamy (plants), were strongly warning the government of the day against the use in arable eastern England of the toxic organochlorines, dieldrin, aldrin and lindane. Their advice was ignored. In 1978, the first National Otter Survey showed that within twenty years of the introduction of these chemicals, less than one hundred otters were left alive in England!

So it is the ongoing neglect of the teachings of ecology which clearly threaten us so much. Our children's future is at risk and, therefore, the very future of mankind itself. It is sad, too, to report we are now seeing far fewer individuals of the stature of those naturalists who were the pioneers of the new understanding of conservation in the '50s and '60s. Today, natural history is dominated by television personalities alongside a government still paying lip service to the real issues.

Are naturalists right, then, in supposing that the wildernesses of the earth are in the long run doomed? Is that a conclusion to which we must ultimately reconcile ourselves? We have and still are transforming wildernesses with homes for human beings by working hand in hand with wild nature, by restricting and guiding her abundance; we preserve her ageless, cyclical processes by bringing into existence countryside in place of a wilderness. It has already been done long ago and perhaps successfully in western Europe. In Britain, wildernesses remain only in those parts of the country which are uninhabitable, either above three thousand feet or between high and low water. Anywhere else there can be a rash of bricks and mortar, on an almost wholly artificial, but often still delightful, countryside. We have, indeed, manipulated our environment.

This process is one thing; it is permissable, safe and calculated to endure, because there the essentials of nature's balance are preserved. But here, since about 1950 and far more in some other parts of the world, particularly in North America, the Amazon Basin and China, nature's moderation is grudgingly regarded. We are still trying even now to improve upon wild nature, as though such a thing were possible, to speed up natural processes which either operated slowly, or not at all and to take short cuts. Then only a long and carefully plotted path will suffice and disasters which we have already witnessed or know to be approaching, will be averted. Maybe, and only then, will our reasonable survival be assured.

Larkin wrote in 1972 and closed "Going Going" with a devastating evocation of the loss of our heritage.

> "And that will be England gone,
> The shadows, the meadows, the lanes,
> The guildhalls, the curved choirs.
> There'll be books; it will linger on
> In galleries; but all that remains
> For us will be concrete and tyres."

The editorial from *The Independent* concludes:

"The guildhalls and choirs mean little enough for many people already. But what is clear now is that there is so much more at risk than Larkin could ever have imagined even three short decades ago. Today we can still share a sense of a natural environment that was once there but which is now slipping away, something mysterious, sacred and wistfully alluring. If we remain complacent it will, for our children and our grandchildren, have totally vanished."

In 2003, Bill McKibben, updating all the statistical information and research, argued what many had suspected and greatly feared but dared not confront.

"... Still the sun rises, still the moon wanes and waxes, but they look down on a planet that means something different, something less than it used to ... this lovely globe ... it has become unbalanced in our short moment on it ... it's mostly us now."

The End of Nature, Bill McKibben 2003

Face to Face – with nature is a reflection on my fifty years of close involvement with the animals and birds of these islands.

I was allowed to keep wild ducks and geese in the garden. The catalyst had been a winter visit to Peter Scott's Severn Wildfowl Trust with my Mum and Dad early in 1950. My paternal grandmother had insisted that we visited the New Grounds, at Slimbridge; she had been captivated by an outside radio broadcast from one of several hides built by Peter Scott in the banks of the River Severn's sea defences. Visitors who tucked into these hides overlooking the Dumbles, the winter pastures, and I was often one of them, would watch at close quarters thousands of European white-fronted geese,

The author with his friend and mentor, Peter Scott, at the opening of the Wildlife Park, in June 1967.

© Jim Hale, 1967; courtesy Mia Hale

teal and wigeon. It was an unbelievable and thrilling sight for an impressionable nine year old. My aspirations had been fired.

I left school, Clifton College in Bristol, worked with the eminent naturalist Philip Wayre in Norfolk during 1961 and 1962 and then went up to Pembroke College, Cambridge, to read Geography. Three years later in June 1965, I created my Wildlife Park and British Nature Centre at Westbury-on-Trym in Bristol. It was opened to the general public in June 1967 by Peter Scott and my early fascination for the world natural was to grow beyond my wildest expectations.

I was working both for, and with, wildlife; I was presenting to, and communicating with, people and with youngsters in particular, illustrating my talks with live but tame exhibits. Through them, I was telling audiences throughout the late '60s and '70s, that all was not well within our countryside. I was stressing that some species, especially those which were at the head of food chains, were flying red danger signals for the environment as a whole. However, and much more importantly, the very same signals were also a warning for another animal species found on planet earth. There are ever-increasing numbers of that species, all of whom are at the head of another food chain. That species, of course, is man himself!

The Dumbles were part of Peter Scott's dream of bringing people close to his beloved wildfowl. His vision was captured in the last painting he ever completed, of the London Wetland Centre at Barnes; 'a wildlife reserve in an urban area where most people live'.
© Peter Partington, 2006. www.peterpartington.fsnet.co.uk

I closed the Wildlife Park in 1978 at the end of my fourteen year lease and left Bristol. I had survived well on fifty thousand visitors a year. I had competed with Bristol Zoo, and with Lord Bath's Safari Park, the Lions of Longleat. However, although on a different scale, my Wildlife Park offered an alternative by providing a more personal interaction between the live exhibits and visitors.

Now, I wanted to pursue a career spelling out crucial wildlife issues, so I kept only the creatures I needed as live exhibits, with one exception. I retained my unique family group of British otters, then the only private, licensed collection in the United Kingdom.

I was fortunate to become only the second person to breed the British otter in the past one hundred years; some thirty-five were parent-reared. I was able to make a significant contribution to a successful release programme, initially carried out in the arable eastern counties of England, from which wild otters had completely disappeared. Trios of unrelated cubs, captive bred but parent-reared were set free under a unique initiative led by Philip and Jeanne Wayre of the Otter Trust at Earsham, Suffolk, meeting all the criteria set by the then Nature Conservancy Council.

In 1999, I self-published *Stormforce – an otter's tale,* the true and remarkable story of an exceptional wild otter cub found by a post-man on Exmoor and called Storm. An award-winning book, it has sold nearly twenty thousand copies nationwide in six editions. Storm's remark, "tell them it's my world too," as she was heard to utter close to the end of her life, (the account of her rescue and struggle for survival is told in the form of conversations with myself), has been read by countless others. I still present that simple but serious message today, and although many of the catastrophic problems that occurred in the decades following the mid-1950s have now been overcome, other new, but similarly long-predicted threats continue to face our and the world's fragile landscapes; and, of course, all living life which depends on those delicate ecosystems.

However, in *Face to Face with nature,* I will only comment on some problems. I will identify a serious issue on which I have a strong opinion; no doubt, the reader will not always agree. If you are now that reader, that young mind then, maybe, just maybe, I will persuade you and your family to adopt a more positive attitude towards the environment. Then the purpose of this book and, indeed, some of my long-term goals will have been achieved.

Some serious issues will emerge amongst my experiences. There are humourous tales, some are sad recollections, but all are true. Nevertheless, they all form an integral part of my life's story.

You see, I want to know in my conscience that because of an enthusiastic and committed presentation to an evening group or to a Year 6 class in a local community junior school, because of someone reading either *Stormforce an otter's tale,* or *Face to Face with nature,* the future of the world's natural wild places have and will become better because I continue to speak and write. Better, in fact, because I informed and wrote again today.

There are times in your life when you pause and realise ... that a day was unforgettable ... that a particular occasion was unbelievable ... and that they were all the more special because of much forward planning and effort. I have enjoyed many such moments and some will play a part in the story I recount in *Face to Face with nature.* Similarly, I have suffered setbacks and disappointments too. I can, and still do forget that tomorrow is always another day ...

However, there have been times when the influence of some individuals has made such an impact that I want to recall the details for others to share; I make no apologies for naming certain characters. Their names and their professions will give the reader an idea of the way my life has evolved; of what, hopefully, others may feel I may have achieved and of what I still hope to accomplish with my family and during my professional working life.

Some people and events will have contributed in apparently insignificant ways. They may not be mentioned by name or specifically again; but, their role and importance will have been greatly relevant in shaping my thoughts, beliefs and efforts over a lifetime. Finally, I hope when *Face to Face* is being read that there is no one who feels that he or she should have deserved a mention. I apologise unreservedly to them should that be the case.

I was unbelievably fortunate to have John 'Jack' and Nancy Chaffe as parents and to grow up within the creative stimulus of a private architect's practice. I enjoyed a loving family life, living successively in three suburbs of the historic and beautiful City of Bristol; at first in Redland, then in Westbury Park and finally, but especially, on the Downs close to Clifton Village.

Through my parents' hard endeavours I was educated at Clifton College. Here I was guided through both the preparatory and senior schools by an array of dedicated and talented teachers in the traditional private school environment of the 1950's. One master in particular, John Kendall-Carpenter, my first XV rugby coach and previously captain of both the Oxford University and England rugby teams, was responsible for giving me life-changing advice. This I followed and it

John and Nancy Chaffe, the author's parents, at the opening of the Wildlife Park, in June 1967

© Jim Hale, courtesy Mia Hale

13

The author, captain of the Clifton College 1st XV alongside the team's coach, John Kendall-Carpenter, former captain of Bath, Cornwall, Oxford University and England.

took me to university. Subsequently, that experience opened new and totally unforeseen horizons.

As an impressionable ten year old I first met the painter and naturalist Peter Scott who became a close friend and mentor. I have witnessed at close hand, and continue to support the expansion of his creation, the Wildfowl and Wetlands Trust at Slimbridge in Gloucestershire; the Trust with its six regional centres throughout the UK is now clearly regarded as one of the world's leading avicultural, conservation and research organisations.

I was privileged to attend Pembroke College, Cambridge, reading for the Geography Tripos. On the fringes of the Fen country, I was close enough to continue my forays to the magical Norfolk coast and its windswept marshes, first enjoyed when working with Philip Wayre.

There were eleven acres of unkempt and long abandoned land in the heart of Westbury upon Trym, a suburb within the city boundaries of Bristol. Here I displayed native animals and birds on such a scale that I created, in '65, and opened in '67, the Wildlife Park and British Nature Centre to the general public. However, long before my fourteen year lease expired, I was trapped by financial limitations. I could not display the animals and birds on the scale which would do them justice. In any case, there was a more pressing message that needed to be told.

So, I began presenting lectures, particularly to younger people; even then, those talks were illustrated with live exhibits. I was reporting that all was not well with planet Earth, that drastic and far-reaching changes were already afoot and were becoming increasingly evident through the decade of the '60s.

Scott, Lockley and Durrell's influence was telling. All three were clearly emphasising the need to understand the greater picture, that no one species can survive unless the places in which it lives, or to which it migrates, are healthy too. I was soon aware therefore, of the simple fact that people everywhere share the very same places as all creatures; that we were already irrevocably damaging those places. I was conscious, as well, that if we continued to treat the environment with increasing disrespect, for societies were coming to think of everything being theirs, we would have little chance, like other creatures at the head of food chains, of surviving too.

My wife Helen, our daughter Olivia and I had the unexpected but unique opportunity, in mid February 1992, to hand-rear an abandoned wild otter cub, called Storm, later of *Stormforce, an otter's tale*. For many years we shared and enjoyed the private and personal life of one of the most endearing creatures found worldwide.

Through that tale, *Face to Face with nature* and my ongoing presentations, I warn others that the future of the planet is under much greater threat than ever before; I stress that we should not just witness that phenomenon, not just treat it as inevitable, and be satisfied and complacent by simply talking about it. The community must create a movement that acts more promptly and seriously with greater morality than at present, far more seriously in fact, than the consumer economy which has over-taken us. We must, therefore, reverse the process known as 'global warming'.

Several miles out in the south-western sea lies the sandstone plateau of Skokholm. Here, Ronald Lockley, the lone naturalist at one with nature, pioneered the first studies of manx shearwaters and storm petrels in the 1930s.

Someone once told me that if and when I reached 50, not only would it be a good time to start living for the present, but also that I would be lucky to count true friends on the fingers of one hand. As the years have slipped by, some very dear companions are, through tragic circumstances, or by their passing, no longer alive to read these words. So, they will never know of my everlasting gratitude for the contribution they made to my family's and to my own life. Sadly, and as often happens, I never did, or was too late, to convey my gratitude to them. Nevertheless, I hope members of their family will read these lines and thus will be aware of my recognition of their precious lives. I refer to them later in *Never in my wildest dreams*.

However, if I am allowed to include Helen and Olivia in the analogy, I can then complete my first list. They would embrace, firstly, John Amor from 'Clifton' years; secondly, Malcolm Sayer from 'Pembroke' times; and thirdly, John Featherstone from the early days of the Wildlife Park; with their respective wives, Sheila, Pat and Judi, they are all aware, without further comment, of how highly I hold their lifelong and enduring friendships.

Face to Face with nature describes just some of the memorable events and significant occasions which have occured since I chose to live in close contact with wild nature from a very early age. I trust you will enjoy the experiences I recall. Then, upon reflection, I hope you will want to visit my favourite wild places and discover the wild creatures that live there for yourself. Most of all, if you are a young person, I hope you will be inpsired to welcome the countryside within your life; and do so, please, to whatever degree is possible given your circumstances. I would be thrilled, too, if you could experience just some of the excitement and fascination of my past fifty years. Maybe, you will also be challenged to find new horizons and different sights and sounds in places to where now, sadly, I will never likely travel. Then, no matter what direction life takes you, I trust you and your family will contribute to the greatest cause of all.

The planet and the natural world must survive. However much we have forgotten, or have been led to believe, that we can afford to be separate from and can live without the Earth's life support systems, the truth is we cannot. We must, all of us, now live in ways that respect the planet and which do not take its natural resources for granted.

We, in the United Kingdom, must continue to influence our European partners, and the United States of America in particular, which has constantly refused to engage in the Kyoto Protocol.

Simultaneously, the same efforts must be made with Japan and the nations of the Indian sub-continent. But it is with the People's Republic of China where, of all places, the need for conservation measures are most apparent. China is flooding the atmosphere with CO_2 emissions on a Californian scale from its use of coal; a coal-fired power station is being built every week for the next seven years.

Finally, we should be turning our attention to Brazil and the Amazon rainforest. In the Independent newspaper for the 23rd of July 2006, one of the world's top ecologists, Dr. Deborah Clark of the University of Minnesota said that "the lock has broken on the Amazon ecosystem and the Amazon is headed in a terrible direction."

Yes, the tasks ahead are enormous!

The time has long since arrived, therefore, when we must not only tell people to love nature and to love life; we, you and I, your neighbour next door and your peers with whom you sit in assembly or in class, must practice new ways of life and new moral responsibilities.

Enjoy *Face to Face with nature,* take the important message it contains forward with you in life and make sure, please, that your carbon footprint is a gentle one.

Chapter One

"Don't move, don't even try to use your binoculars."

Three redshank, *Tringa totanus* and a pair of dunlin, *Calidris alpuria*
seek the tide's edge

Water, or rather an excess or lack of it, continues to play a major impact on breeding wetland birds.

Saltmarshes, the special habitat for a rich variety of breeding and wintering wildfowl and waders, occur where there are no strong tides or currents preventing sediment settling. Salt tolerant plants, like eel-grass and glasswort, help trap the silt and sand carried by the tides.

The UK is continuing to lose coastal saltmarshes as well as inland wet meadows at a dramatic pace; the latter are the breeding grounds of redshank, lapwing and shelduck ... meadow pipit and skylark ...

courtesy RSPB 'Birds' Magazine and 'Environment Today', 2006

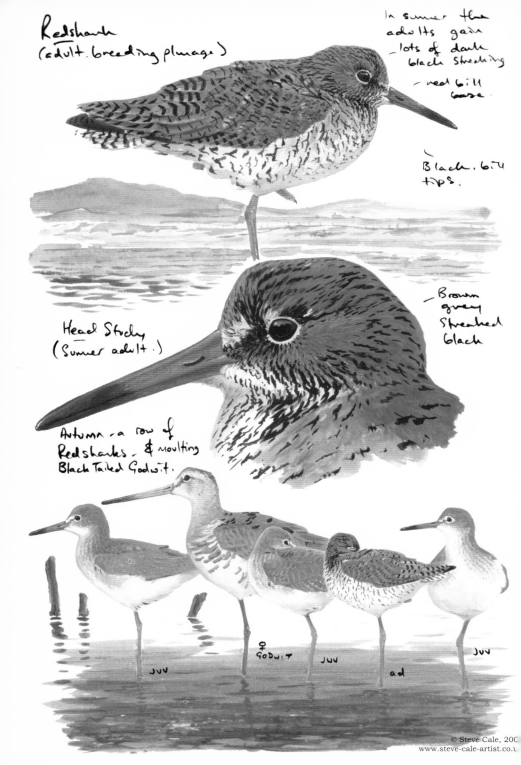

Redshank
(adult. breeding plumage.)

In summer the
adults gain
- lots of dark
black streaking
- red bill
base.

Black. bill
tips.

Head Study
(Summer adult.)

Brown
grey
streaked
black

Autumn - a row of
Redshanks - & moulting
Black Tailed Godwit.

JUV

♀
GODWIT

JUV

ad

JUV

© Steve Cale, 200
www.steve-cale-artist.co.t

F*ace-to-Face with nature* begins a long while ago on the evening before my eighth birthday. I was living in suburban Bristol.

It had been a typical late November day, grey and overcast with low cloud and a constant heavy drizzle. Around six o'clock it was raining even harder, with the downpour beating against the kitchen windows. I was having tea with my mother and father. Next door, a small utility room served as the back entrance to our bungalow in Cranbrook Road, Redland. It was also an outside larder, a home for wellington boots, and the mangle was kept there for hand-wringing the weekly washing. Outside, steep steps led towards the back garden; across a large sloping lawn was a small orchard full of mature apple and pear trees; beyond the hedge boundary were cultivated allotments.

My father was an architect and surveyor; he had qualified in the mid 1930s after matriculating at Colston's School. My paternal grandmother had immediately articled him with Meredith, the Bristol architect, whose city centre offices were in Denmark St, and almost 'next door' to the Bristol Hippodrome Theatre. John 'Jack' Chaffe had left school at the time of the Great Depression and Grandma Chaffe, widowed with three children before the eldest, my father, was five years of age had scrimped and saved every penny possible as licensee of the Avon Packet public house in Coronation Road, Bedminster. The business was close to the WD and HO Wills tobacco factories and to the Albion shipyards within the heart of Bristol's dockland. Today from the Avon Packet, you can see the tall masts of the SS Great Britain as she lies in her dock, restored after her return from the Falkland Islands. Much of the trade in the

Redshank, *Tringa totanus*

pub's bars was conducted 'on tick'. Nevertheless, Florence Chaffe gave both her sons, Dad and his younger brother, my uncle Ronnie, the best possible start in life.

My mother, Nancy, née Machin, had fallen for the aspiring architect at a very young age. She was trained as a beautician and had worked in Jones's. This major department store in Broadmead was also close to Bristol's bustling city centre, with the docks and River Avon at its heart. Both brothers were sportsmen; Jack played rugby for Bristol; his brother, a year younger and fresh from Cotham Grammar School, represented Gloucestershire at county level in athletics, swimming and rugby. They lived and enjoyed life to the full and there was no doubt that my mother was attracted to their wicked sense of fun and mischief. This November night was further proof of that.

The aspiring architect and the beautician; the author's parents, Nancy and Jack Chaffe, in Bristol in the mid-1930s.

"What on earth was that noise?" my mother suddenly exclaimed.

In the austere post-war years of continued rationing we might have been eating toast smeared with beef dripping with salt or marmite to flavour; another favourite was cockles with vinegar. Most times, however, it was plain bread and margarine with home-made jam, or beetroot and tomatoes. However, boiled eggs often featured and laid by our own free range chickens, too. That fact should have given me a clue.

For a while we had been visiting a farm close to the village of Pucklechurch which, today, lies amongst the concreted suburbia blanketing vast acreages north of Bristol. Dad was clearly involved with the new construction work on the farm but arranged his appointments at weekends so Mum and I could accompany him in our little black Austin Seven. Suddenly, I was close to farm animals and birds, about which I had only previously read in my favourite 'Romany' books. Imagine my amazement as I witnessed the hand-milking of the herd of dairy cows, and of being allowed to search for and collect the hens' eggs. My treat, however, was being entrusted with a pail of wheat and taking it across the fields to a pond.

A great bedlam of noise, accompanied by the flapping of wings, would occur before the ducks and geese finally gathered around me. They appeared trusting but, in truth, were quite wary. I was there perhaps once a month, and then only for an hour or two at most. The flock was rarely in touch with the everyday activities around the farmyard and I never quite managed to persuade them to feed from my hand. I longed to achieve that.

The water, constantly fed by a stream, was full of natural life and always had some of its surface flecked with duckweed, especially in summertime. The farmer only needed to supplement the birds' diet in the depths of winter. There were wild duck, too; several would always 'spring' as I approached. I presumed they were mallard. There must have been moorhens, even water rails, and herons and kingfishers surely visited. Pied wagtails were always around; the 'greys' and the 'yellows' were summer visitors. At seven years of age, I was unaware of many species and frightened them away as I chased enthusiastically across the field to the water's edge.

We had returned home on one occasion with half a dozen young pullets, three each of Rhode Island Red and Light Sussex. Mum had, reluctantly, given in to my repeated requests, having been finally persuaded that freshly-laid and gathered eggs would be a real bonus to our everyday meals.

I had been put in charge of the chickens. We would bring home whole wheat from the farm in huge hessian sacks. We fed a 'mash' too, encouraging the birds to lay regularly; there was always a saucepan on the stove in which the left-overs from the kitchen and our meals were boiled. I once caused my mother great embarrassment at Pont's, the grocers on close-by Cheltenham Road. I let slip that we did not eat the black pudding bought with the last of our meat coupons, but rather that it was added to the chickens' mash!

"There it goes again, d'ye hear?" my mother exclaimed.

"I didn't hear anything, Nancy," Dad replied, but rather too casually. He then winked at me.

"Well I did. I'm not stupid, you know. Don't you try and fool me." Mum was always quick to respond.

Meanwhile, there was an uneasy silence. Suddenly I heard the noise, and this time it was very distinctive, very loud, and very close. There could be no mistake, and one duck could never have made that much noise!

There was no doubt that my mother was attracted to Jack Chaffe's sense of fun

"I know that sound; that's ducks, isn't it, flamin' ducks! I told you not to get them. Where are you going to put them anyway? Have you thought of that? No!" Mum was now on her high horse.

I was still looking at Dad and he winked again.

"They were meant to be a surprise for David's birthday tomorrow," he started, "but I couldn't leave them outside in this weather."

"They're ducks aren't they? I thought ducks were supposed to like water. So where are they then?" Mum was off again.

"They're just next door ... in the back porch. Shall we look at them now or leave it to the morning? They're quite safe in there for now." Wisely, Dad was being rather cautious.

A long silence followed.

Eventually Mum spoke. "Well, alright, I suppose it would be a pity to spoil tomorrow. But they'll have to stay in there for now, and don't expect me to feed and water them. It's always me that's left holding the baby."

"... looking after my Aylesburys and Khaki Campbell ducks, and the chickens, of course, dominated my daily routine ..."

That was typical of my mother. Initially she would always reject an idea, but given time she would always resign herself to the inevitable. Then she would throw herself wholeheartedly into a project, many times doing just what she had previously said she wouldn't do 'in a month of Sundays'.

I was so excited I didn't sleep much that night; in any case the ducks quacked constantly. We thought that they would be frightened of the dark in a strange place so a light was left on. The farmer told us later that we should have done exactly the opposite for any peace and quiet. However, I would never have imagined then the many times there were to be in the future when I would experience similar feelings before, or just after, the arrival of a new creature.

So, looking after my Aylesburys and Khaki Campbell ducks, and the chickens, of course, dominated my daily routine. I went to see them several times a day, and they became very tame. I would feel the hens pecking for the grains of wheat on the palm of my hands, whilst the ducks would tickle my skin as they shovelled with their more cumbersome beaks. I became very fond of the wild birds that would gather around the scattered feeding places. The garden's robins picked up the worms as I dug the pen to freshen the soil and I was forever baling out and refilling with fresh water the two ducks' baths. Outside the breakfast room window, we hung strands of bacon rind and halves of coconuts for the tits. Chaffinches, blackbirds and song thrushes fed on the food we scattered on the ground, and I first learnt the secretive ways of wrens. Years later, Storm's wild mother would rely on their inquisitive ways and constant chatter. Starlings and house sparrows were everywhere and also a common sight on Bristol's streets. A local brewery, George's, had many horse-drawn delivery vehicles; they were an impressive sight in the daily city-centre life of post-war Bristol. The overspill of oats and barley from the nosebags provided a constant source of food, particularly in wintertime. Horses have long-since disappeared from our streets; the house sparrow is in decline but research tells us that, although primarily a grain feeder, sparrows' youngsters need live food during the first week of their lives. Years ago, that source would have come from the piles of dung.

Our garden was much more than my playground; it was where I formed my first strong attachments to the natural living world; I learnt, too, that if you keep animals and birds you have a responsibility for their ongoing care and well-being every day of the year, whatever the circumstances. Maybe, I was realising that the more time you spend with them, then the greater their response and one's reward, and so the more magical the relationship.

However, there were setbacks, as when another Rhode Island chicken arrived with her two newly hatched chicks. We had experienced no problems previously so promptly released the new family. All seemed to be going well. But sadly, forty-eight hours later, both chicks were dead, drowned in one of the small duck ponds. I remember feeling devastated. It was a lack of forethought, we did not spare enough time to be aware of potential problems. We were all upset; nevertheless, the harsh reality of the very fine line between life and death for all living creatures was brought home for the very first time by that tragedy. Sadly, it wasn't to be the last occasion but, sometimes, unforeseen circumstances would prove beyond my control.

Bristol, as so much of post-war Britain, was changing rapidly. I left my kindergarten, briefly attended Bristol Grammar School, before transferring to Clifton College Preparatory School. Rationing was to come to an end, horses and trams were to vanish from the streets of Bristol and significantly, given my growing interest in birds, the Bristol Waterworks Company was creating a new reservoir in the River Chew valley, south of Bristol. It was needed to meet the demands of a rapidly expanding urban population and my father, as an architect, would be partly responsible for the disappearance of many hundreds of green acres on the city outskirts. Did constantly seeing that loss at close quarters, for I was forever on various construction sites, play an important role, 'sow the seeds' as it were, in shaping my thoughts and feelings?

However and much more significantly, Lt Commander Peter Scott had, in November 1946, created the Severn Wildfowl Trust on part of the Berkeley Estates in Gloucestershire. The grounds were close to the River Severn, alongside the Berkeley New Decoy, and adjacent to the Dumbles, meadows flooded only by the highest of the Severn tides and grazed in summer by countless sheep. In autumn and winter, thousands of European white-fronted geese would overwinter from their Arctic Russian breeding grounds in Novaya Zemlya, a thousand miles north of Moscow.

Neither I or my parents could have possibly appreciated the impact of those regular weekend journeys along the A38. One not so surprising consequence is that *Face-to-Face with nature* is to be launched nationally at the Slimbridge Centre of the Wildfowl and Wetlands Trust in 2007, the year after the 60th anniversary year of the Trust's creation. Secondly, I am presently sitting alongside four Greenland white-fronted geese. One young gander is determined to unravel the laces on my shoes as I sit cross-legged in front of him; another young female is preening vigorously whilst still contriving to stare at me. She is Kaitok, an Inuit name, meaning 'Rowena' and used by the Kognuit Eskimos. Her photograph is on the front cover.

Another birthday present a couple of years later, was to provide a similar catalyst to the way my life was being fashioned and which had been kindled by those first farmyard stock.

November the 19th is a very special date for me and nineteen a very lucky number, too. Freebooter, ridden by Pat Taaffe, was drawn number 19 when winning the Grand National in 1951. My father had placed a shilling to win on the horse, which I had randomly selected, at odds of twenty to one. My first National Premium Bonds winner was a ticket whose combined reference numbers added to nineteen. Finally, the letter confirming my acceptance to read geography at Pembroke College, Cambridge, was written on the 19th of the month.

Shortly after lunch on this November Saturday, we were in a semi-detached house on Filton Avenue in north-west Bristol, in response to an advert in one of the Bristol or regional newspapers. The houses here overlook the extensive sports grounds that still belong to British Aerospace, then the Bristol Aircraft Corporation. It was at the B.A.C. that my father had worked as a designer and draughtsman during and just after the war. With my parents I had watched the maiden test flights of the giant Brabazon passenger airliner navigated by the company's chief test pilot, Bill Pegg. She was the prototype for the 'Whispering Giant', the smaller and sleeker Britannia. My uncle, Bill Machin, my mother's brother, was one of the chief electricians in the Britannia's construction team. He was much involved in the urgent need to discover the causes behind the forced landing of a prototype on the mudbanks of the River Severn in February 1954. Exposed to the bitter cold whilst working around the clock during that search for vital clues, Uncle Bill contracted pneumonia. Tragically, he passed away, prematurely, a few months later.

Squadron Leader R I 'Chipper' Chaffe, one of the 'Few', who served the 'Many' by fighting in the Battle of Britain.

In the early stages of the Second World War my late uncle Ronald (Ronnie) Chaffe had flown his Hurricane fighter several times into RAF Filton where Beaufighters were under construction. The first occasion coincided with his stationing at RAF Aldergrove, outside of Belfast; 43 squadron were defending the Harland and Woolf shipyards against long-range German bombers.

Ronnie flew in over the River Severn past Avonmouth docks, in broad daylight and unannounced. This really did put the cat among the pigeons! Air-raid sirens were activated around Filton as the lone

fighter approached. The production line workers rapidly scattered for the underground shelters and bunkers, as did my father and the rest of the drawing office staff. However, the all-clear was sounded once the Hurricane had been identified as 'friendly'. Imagine my father's utter disbelief, yet sheer delight, when he suddenly heard a very familiar voice announcing, "My name is Flying Officer Chaffe, and I have come to see a fellow called Chaffe." Ronnie was carrying a hold-all full of Irish butter for our family and under his other arm, as always, his mascot, a black Irish water spaniel.

Ronnie, Hurricane fighter pilot, was in combat over Czechoslovakia and Warsaw, Poland, from the start of hostilities, in 1939.

Over many years I can recall the tears, the sadness in my father's face, during the November Remembrance Sunday services. He was clearly tormented, remembering his late brother. Maybe he was recalling those few special occasions when Ronnie could visit, and the sense of foreboding he clearly experienced every time his brother departed Filton. My father described a typical departure only once; the details remain vivid.

Wearing his flying jacket and with his faithful dog as his companion, he would always circle one last time after take-off. He would make one final, very, very low-level attack run over the 'drome, and frighten the living daylights out of those watching. Then he would bank away to the north-west and Wales, eventually crossing the Irish Sea to Belfast, and his squadron's base. He would continually wave goodbye, only closing the cockpit canopy finally as he disappeared into the distance. Squadron Leader R.I. 'Chipper' Chaffe, sadly already widowed, was killed in action over Valetta Harbour, Malta, in February 1942. I was three months of age and he had seen me just the once.

I left the Filton Avenue house that afternoon excitedly clutching a pair of second-hand French Stereor 12x35 mm field glasses. The immediate question was where to look at some birds. My father took the decision. He wouldn't say exactly where we were going which added to my excitement, other than the journey would be brief. We

As the black-headed gulls came into their full breeding plumage, the redshanks would shortly leave for their summer pastures.

© Peter Partington, 2006. www.peterpartington.fsnet.co.uk

drove along the Southmead Road, past the highly acclaimed hospital, through part of Henleaze and into the old village of Westbury-on-Trym, nowadays a suburb of Bristol. We passed the Clifton Rugby Club ground in Eastfield Road where in the mid-sixties I was to play for the first XV as a back-row flanker. Close to the ground was the almost invisible turning into Chock Lane, a narrow access leading into the secluded Trym valley. Here eleven acres of woodland and paddocks, part of the National Children's Homes Holmwood Estate, became the location for my Wildlife Park and British Nature Centre, which Peter Scott would open to the general public in June 1967. The Clifton Rugby ground and the adjacent open spaces, that were also sports fields belonging to the Queen Elizabeth Hospital School in Bristol have now, but inevitably I suppose, been covered in homes. The valley that was the Wildlife Park for nearly fifteen years remains relatively unscathed: however, as an open space resource for those living in the nearby urban sprawl, reflecting Bristol's massive expansion in the past fifty years, it is a blatant and sad example of a missed opportunity. More importantly, its potential as a 'next door' nature reserve for Westbury upon Trym's junior school, which is not five minutes walk away from the park's entrance, has also been neglected. At the end of my lease, how much more relevant it would have been for the Bristol City Council and its Education Authority to combine with the NCH to harness the natural environment through which the river Trym flowed. This could have, and should still be complimenting youngsters' non-curricular

Larger waders, oyster catchers and curlew, were easy to recognise alongside the shelducks.

© Peter Partington, 2006. www.peterpartington.fsnet.co.uk

work in Key Stages 1 and 2. Given the density of people living nearby in north-west Bristol, at least a dozen junior schools would now be sharing a unique and remarkable resource.

That Saturday afternoon, my anticipation was soon answered. We parked close to Sea Mills where the same River Trym finally enters the tidal River Avon. Over a thousand years before, the Romans had established a settlement on the high ground nearby. This provided a good vantage point from which to overlook their moored trading galleys, and to spot visitors approaching upstream from the Horseshoe Bend. Downstream, in the little harbour of Pill, were the pilot cutters which journey the River Severn and the Bristol

Channel as far out as the Steep and Flat Holms; at this point the pilots board the inbound ocean freighters heading for Avonmouth and today's vast Royal Portbury Dock.

We made our way under the railway bridge which carried the Great Western suburban railway line from Bristol Temple Meads to Avonmouth Docks and, eventually, to Severn Beach some miles beyond. Now, we were on the towpath alongside the river.

This stretch of the river Avon was to become a special place. I would return time and time again over many years. Even if the tide was full, with no expanse of exposed mud for the birds, there was always the alternative sight of passing ships, making their way to and from the City docks. Cargo vessels and coasters of all shapes and sizes, flying flags of many nations arriving from and departing to, European, Scandinavian and Mediterranean ports. Bristol also had regular direct links to Irish and Scottish harbours.

I still remember the names of some 'regulars'; they became friends. The *Findhorn*, the *Brora*, and the *Annan* traded to and from Glasgow and Belfast, as did the more modern Coast Line vessels. All these berthed in that arm of the docks that stretched deep into the city centre. The *Pluto*, *Cato*, *Juno* and *Echo*, the Bristol Steam Navigation Company ships, were inevitably alongside the wharves overlooked by St Mary Redcliffe church. Amidst all these ships, there would be John Brown's tugs pulling strings of barges laden with freight brought from faraway lands across the world's oceans by cargo vessels berthed in Avonmouth.

The Elder Dempster boats would have carried hard woods from West Africa, the Clan Line ships tobacco and spices from Mombasa and East African ports, and the Shaw Savill Line freighters frozen meat from Australia and New Zealand. The most striking, with white superstructures and yellow funnels, were the Elder and Fyffe's boats with passengers, mails and bananas from the Caribbean. Whatever the cargoes, they finally reached their eventual destinations in Bristol or the Midlands either by rail, by canal via Sharpness and ever increasingly by road.

I was looking at every bird that moved, such was my curiosity. There were gulls everywhere, hundreds of them, very pale with red-brown legs and bills; they were black-headed, although not displaying dark chocolate heads; some had a bold black ear spot, others, presumably youngsters, had ginger-brown upperparts and yellowish legs. There was a continual commotion as they gathered by a sewage outfall pipe where some of Bristol's untreated sewage was being endlessly discharged into the ebbing tide. Carrion crows, all black in sharp contrast, but with similarly strident calls, were apparently the only other birds around, as they painstakingly sorted the detritus on the river's edge.

We were sitting astride a log that must have been deposited a good while previously after an extremely high spring or autumn tide. Now deeply embedded, it was well hidden in the tussock grass along with years of accumulated flotsam and jetsam.

Suddenly, with rapid wingbeats and a long gliding flight, a small brownish bird with outstretched legs alighted at the water's edge. Immediately, it stood alert, right in front of us and just a few yards away. The bird appeared anxious, frequently bobbing its head as if it was looking for companions.

"Don't move", my father whispered, "don't even try to use your binoculars."

We could clearly see the bird's markings and colours with the naked eye. It was a delicately proportioned bird, with sleek and soft brown plumage, so different to the massed ranks of gulls. The sharp bill was partly coloured red and the long red legs were an orange-red against the red-brown of the gulls. Neither of us had a clue to its identity. Then, all at once, two more individuals arrived in a hurry, flighting in as if from nowhere, across the sluggish tidewater. There were spontaneous greetings between the birds, distinctive but plaintive calls, as excited recognition and conversation took place. Soon, all three were probing the wet mud for small crustaceans and worms. Later, we spotted both the broad white edging to their wings and also their white rumps, especially whenever the birds flew away from us.

We heard and spotted several more in the next hour; some birds appeared to be regularly criss-crossing the river, but our threesome stayed close. It was low water and with dusk and an enveloping damp November mist closing in, we turned our backs on the river. We could still hear the birds' distinctive calls as we passed under the railway bridge in the gathering darkness.

"Redshanks, they were redshanks," I called excitedly to my parents from my bedroom. I rushed into the kitchen, clutching my Observers Book of Birds. "Look, on page one hundred and sixty-three, they've got to be redshanks," and with great enthusiasm, I read them all the information.

I watched the River Avon birds as frequently as I could through-out that winter. Sometimes we paused up-river within sight of Brunel's Clifton Suspension Bridge and the lock-gated entrance to the Cumberland Basin, the initial anchorage for the City docks. On other occasions, we used the same towpath and crossed the same railway line, but would arrive closer to the river's mouth and the Severn estuary. There were different, larger gulls, herring and great black-backs and I recognised other waders just by their size, shape and colour. Three were easy; curlew, oyster-catcher and lapwing. However, there were many other grey or brown individuals behaving in typical wader fashion, feeding busily on the mud or running fast at the tide's edge. It was frustrating and disappointing when having discovered a flock, to see them taking rapid and zig-zagging flight, twisting and turning across the estuary before alighting again, this time usually out of range of easy identification, and becoming 'lost' by intermingling with others of a very similar shape and colour. I needed an 'expert' who could have pinpointed the critical features of each species; shape and length of bills, wing and rump patterns and distinctive flight calls and behaviour.

I now know that I was looking at mixed flocks of grey and golden plover, godwit, knot and dunlin. Undoubtedly there must have been rarer birds, but I will never know what I saw and failed to recognise. Even today, this very afternoon, as I write by Halspill Creek close by the Torridge Estuary here in north Devon, I still struggle. Yes, the regulars are a short distance away, but are the sandpipers back from Africa and only briefly refuelling whilst 'on passage', Common, Green or even Wood?

Then, around Eastertime, the redshanks had disappeared. We searched hard on several occasions, dropping in consecutively on our favourite locations along the river, but to no avail.

"They're supposed to be resident," I explained to my father after reading the Observer's Book for the umpteenth time, as well as checking through another reference book he had borrowed from the library, no less than the *Handbook of British Birds*.

"Look, I think I know of an area where they might possibly be," he suggested one evening. He had appreciated my disappointment over the redshanks' departure. "Next weekend I'll take you. Meanwhile, I'll have to find out, ask around, on how best to get there. But we'll give it a go. What do you say?"

"Is it far away? Go on tell me." I pressed him to reveal all.

"It's a place called Portbury Wharf. You reach it via Sheepway. You need to find the right lane before walking out across the fields. I've heard you can get out as far as the Severn Estuary."

"Sounds great," I replied, "I can't wait."

We did find the appropriate lane, parked at its seaward end and by climbing a five bar gate, followed a narrow track lined by black-thorn hedges in full blossom. Rough pastures led away into the distance. There were saltmarsh ewes with recently born lambs and to make progress we were continually jumping the drainage ditches that randomly criss-crossed these early summertime pastures.

The first birds we put up were a pair of shelducks. They were surprised by our presence and previously, no doubt, were only used to the farmer who visited these remote fields. The shelducks kept clear

Royal Portbury Dock, where the Port and the Hawk and Owl Trust have worked together to ensure that Barn Owls have continued to hunt and breed throughout its expansion. In 2005, Bristol Zoo introduced Water Voles to the rhynes inside the dock.

1991

"It is a wide and empty marsh ... not changed that much in the last few centuries ... humming with the far calls of a thousand sheep ...

The pastures would be alive with the courting calls of redshank, shelduck and skylark in the nesting month of May ... teal and wigeon, mewing like cats, tuck in behind the high sea wall on chilly winter evenings ...

At that moment a white form suddenly ghosted out of the lengthening shadows .. it was a barn owl and a first for the boy; then just as quickly as it had appeared, it was gone, floating away across the marsh in the gathering dusk ...

The marsh became a regular 'must' for the young boy naturalist; he began to feel the glitter and sheen of creeping tide, the drift of suaeda pods on summer water and the sea wind running like mice through singing summer grasses.

2003

Twenty years later, the marsh has sadly received its final calling for it is now the site of the new West Dock for the Port of Bristol Authority. The wildness of that marsh has gone to be replaced by an artificial scene created by earth removers and giant bulldozers. The story behind the death sentence of that marsh could be repeated a thousand times throughout Western Europe.

David Chaffe, the boy naturalist, describes Portbury Wharf in 1950.

from the introduction (1973) to
And Let the Earth Listen © David Chaffe,

Stop Press: The Port has just installed three two megawatt wind turbines which will provide for all of its electrical needs when the wind is blowing, (equivalent to the consumption for 5000 homes).

of the reed-fringed ditches, calling loudly as they swung out over the distant seawall to the wide mudflats of the estuary.

"That's definitely a pair," I called excitedly, "looks as tho' they are planning to nest nearby. This could be a good area."

I didn't realise then the drake had probably been escorting the duck to or from the vicinity of her nesting burrow; she may have been briefly off her clutch of eggs for a quick wash and feed. We had already seen plenty of rabbits and I also didn't know then that shelducks favour disused rabbit burrows as nest-sites.

"Maybe it would be best if we stayed here," suggested Dad, "we'll only go on disturbing the shelducks and any other birds too. If we just make ourselves scarce, we'll see what turns up."

My father, although in no way a bird-watcher, had just hit the nail on the head. The secret is always, of course, to sit tight and let 'whatever' come to you. The times I have ignored that and jeopardised success are far too numerous to recall.

So we stayed, and what a fantastic couple of hours. We moved to lose ourselves against one of the occasional lines of fencing which divided, as far as the eye could see, the grazing rights of these wharf pastures. From our vantage point we could see the various activities in many narrow but deep drainage ditches, but we concentrated our attention on the two close by. We spotted a female mallard; she was 'quacking' anxiously; clearly her brood of ducklings was nearby. A pair of moorhens looked similarly nervous and distracted as they moved in and out of the tall rushes. The first thrill, however, was a pair of sparrow-like birds, clinging to the tall stems of the nearby phragmites. One had a black head and throat with a pure white neck band; reed buntings, a first.

"What was that?" I suddenly whispered, "I know that call."

We waited, anxiously scouring the vast expanse of tussocky grass. We saw nothing. Maybe ten minutes later, there were the calls again, obviously from two birds, but that second occasion allowed us to pinpoint a specific area. Then, there were heads jerking distinctively and more uneasy cries. Finally, we saw the pair flying together along the length of a drainage ditch and eventually out of sight. It was time to leave my precious redshanks.

The sun had, for a while now, slipped behind the Brecon Beacons and we had a long walk to the car. But we made a promise to come back, soon.

Go back we did and on several occasions, too. We took a khaki blanket to help disguise our presence and on our fourth visit, we watched the female redshank both leave and return to her nest in her chosen tussock. She had laid her clutch just yards from where we had first seen the birds a month previously. We glanced briefly at, and photographed the nest, with its four heavily blotched eggs lying deep in the fine grass-lined cup.

Then, we decided to leave the redshanks alone. I hoped their youngsters would survive; we never did see the shelducklings, the young reed-buntings or even the brood of skylarks at whose father we had marvelled as he sang ever higher in the early summer skies. Nevertheless, we always saw the mallard ducklings and the young moorhen chicks; in mid-June, at the time of our last visit, both broods were well grown and would, most likely, now reach maturity.

By early September I was regularly watching the redshanks again; they were back around Sea Mills and were, as always, working the tide's edge.

Chapter Two

"There are Bantams Everywhere!"

Greenland White-fronted Geese, *Anser albifrons flavirostris*
© John Threlfall 2007
www.johnthrelfall.co.uk

"There was a gaggle of five geese. Greenland white-fronts;
definitely an adult pair with their three youngsters."

In 1937, Peter Scott was given two geese by a friend, David Haigh Thomas, on the latter's return from West Greenland. Both birds had yellow beaks, instead of the usual pink, and were also darker than the European white-fronted geese, (*Anser a albifrons*), that migrate to UK wetlands from northern Russia.

Together with drawings and photographs and the skin of a bird shot out of the wintering flocks on the Wexford Sloughs in Ireland in 1947, Peter Scott and Christopher Dalgety named the species *Anser albifrons flavirostris* - the goose 'white-fronted and yellow-billed'.

It was first reported to the scientific world at the 475th meeting of the British Ornithologists Club, on the 17th March 1948.

courtesy of Paul Walkden, biographer to the late Sir Peter Scott, 2006

In 1987, the Home Rule Authorities of Greenland designated eleven areas of the country as 'Ramsar Sites', areas of outstanding international importance as habitat for wildfowl, and named after the town of Ramsar in Iran, where the original agreement was drawn up in 1971. Five of these, covering 7000 square kilometres were the summer home then for 9000 Greenland white-fronted geese, 40 per cent of the world's population.

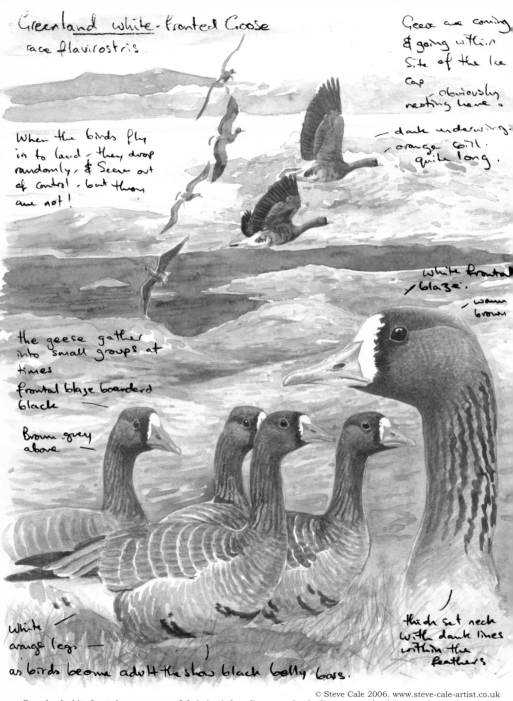

Greenland white-fronted Goose
race flavirostris.

Geese are coming
& going within
site of the Ice
Cap   obviously
nesting here.

— dark underwing
– orange bill.
quite long.

When the birds fly
in to land - they drop
randomly, & seem out
of control - but they
are not!

white frontal
blaze.

warm
brown

the geese gather
into small groups at
times
frontal blaze boardered
black   —

Brown grey
above

white —
orange legs —

thick set neck
with dark lines
within the
feathers

as birds become adult they show black belly bars.

Greenland white-fronted geese on one of their Arctic breeding grounds, the Naternaq wetland in central west Greenland.

"A magical place, home to some of 6000 white-fronts in just 1500 square kilometres, ... red-throated divers, long-tailed ducks and red-necked phalaropes ... a vast swampy landscape, a mass of creamy-white lakes full of suspended glacial sediments and hooching with plant nutrients."
© Dr. Tony Fox, The Wildfowl & Wetlands Trust, Slimbridge, Gloucestershire, May 1989

I had no real problems with my wildfowl collection in the back garden of our Bristol home, which was just a stone's throw from Brunel's Suspension Bridge and the unique Clifton Observatory.

My father employed trainee draughtsmen in his architect's practice in our large Victorian house in which we also lived, and which had remained empty for a decade since World War II. Companies also leased office space. The Guinness Park Royal accommodation included a visitors' lounge with an en-suite bar to promote their product. Every Christmas we were given a very large, richly spiced, Christmas pudding and an equally bountiful Stilton cheese, both of which we could still be eating at Easter-time! The company's annual New Year's party entertained the stars of the Christmas pantomime from the Bristol Hippodrome Theatre. I can recall my parents meeting George Formby, Jimmy Edwards and a very young and exciting newcomer, Bruce Forsyth.

Other office space was at the rear of the property; the staff could watch my birds and being continually distracted, were forever opening the windows to feed them. This continuous rapport, and many clearly had favourites, encouraged some ducks and geese to become very tame. The sloping garden was bounded on either side by high walls; the offices were one boundary and an abandoned two storey mews coach house at the foot of the garden completed the square. Attached to the latter was a large, dilapidated timber-framed greenhouse where two gnarled grape vines fruited every year. It was in here the future success of my collection would evolve and where I was to spend so much of my spare time.

At the time of my first visit to Ceredigion, the number of red kites, *Milvus milvus*, quartering the remote upland bog of Cors Caron, could have been counted on the fingers of one hand ...

© Photolibrary Wales. www.photolibrarywales.com

Disasters were few and far between. We were close to the Downs, which is still an unspoilt and vast open space to the north-west of the city. Striking features are parallel lines of mature horse chestnut trees cutting across the open grassland, and scrub woodland with dense cover which borders the limestone cliffs and gullies of the steep gorge of the River Avon. We expected problems with the resident foxes, frequently spotting individuals, especially at night-time, as they hunted their territories. However, it appeared that they were either finding enough natural food or the garden's walls were too great an obstacle.

Nevertheless, there was to be one major tragedy.

Birthdays were red letter days. On this occasion I knew I was being given a pair of North American Cinammon Teal. They had been reared in the late Terry Jones' collection on the Leckford Estates close to Stockbridge in Hampshire; his birds thrived on the crystal clear waters of chalk streams feeding into the River Test. The ducks had been railed to Bristol Temple Meads station, and my father had then released them into an aviary which we used for birds that needed to be isolated; individuals might go off colour, be bullied, perhaps during the inevitable squabbling at feeding time, and a lame bird would need time and space to recover. I was to meet the teal, albeit briefly, for the first time early the next morning.

I couldn't believe my eyes as I approached the pen. Both birds had been torn to shreds; amongst all the scattered carnage and chaos of bloodied feathers and ripped limbs, I could still pick out the birds' blue speculum feathers. These contrasted so vividly with the deep russet-red plumage of the drake. Some creature had squeezed under the wire of the enclosure which, sadly, had only been fixed flush to the ground, a mistake I have avoided ever since.

What sadistic creature had simply toyed with the birds and yet not eaten them? A fox would have surely taken one away even if it had beheaded the other as well. Immediately, we were concerned for the safety of the rest of the collection. So, drastic and prompt action was necessary and a plan was hatched.

The chickens, whose home was in the greenhouse, were boxed. However, one bird was left behind, very secure in a coop. In the attached run, there was a dish of strong-smelling liver. The greenhouse was left open. A length of strong twine, tied around the door handle, fed up to the first floor window of the empty coach house. Two lads from the offices, and all the staff had been particularly upset by the loss of the ducks, had volunteered to wait and spring the trap on any intruder that might return. They planned to stay all night. However, there was no need to have made such elaborate plans. Barely an hour after darkness the predator returned, and from where we shall never know. Immediately it fell for the bait and the door was pulled shut. It was no fox, as expected.

"Gotcha! Biggest moggy I've seen," were the first words I heard.

We had a helluva job catching the cat. He really was elusive and vicious with a flat wide head; we were certain he was feral, living rough on the nearby Downs. His first visit had sadly coincided with the teal's first night with us. They had stood no chance.

The beast was eventually secured in a tea-chest and taken away. Dad was gone a long time; he never did tell me where this awful character was released, but his new territory was certainly a very long way from my collection!

The greenhouse was to play a very important role. For some time I had been finding out as much information as possible about breeding waterfowl and I wanted to hatch and rear any youngsters in its sheltered confines. However, I fell into the trap of not adequately planning ahead. A local greengrocer had given me grape barrels which I half-buried in clumps of reeds and rushes, they provided the essential cover for would-be nesting ducks.

I cobbled together ladders to give access to other boxes secured in the apple trees. These potential homes were for the Carolina wood ducks, natives of the coniferous fir forests of North America. The Carolinas, along with my mallards and red-crested pochards, would be the earliest layers. I had planned for the mallards to hatch and rear their own clutches; nevertheless, none of us realised just how early in the year the birds would lay. By early March complete clutches of eggs were ready to be incubated. I know now that this was because the ponds, already well sheltered, were bathed all winter long in artificial light radiating from the offices. The modern, for those days in the mid-fifties, fluorescent lights were continually switched on in autumn and winter from three thirty until half past five, if not later, by the time the cleaners had finished. We were unnaturally stimulating the onset of spring; we were unaware of the imbalance we were creating to the birds' time-clocks.

"Silkie-cross bantams," I would repeatedly say to my father. "Broody silkies, that's what we need."

There were countless occasions when my mother, on greeting me home from school, would add, "and you've no idea how many phone calls your father has made again today looking for flippin' broodies. It's taking over the office." Meanwhile, in the old greenhouse where I was to keep my flock of potential foster-mothers, we had laid turf over the bare earth of the original seed beds. Previously, I had spent hours removing years of accumulated weed growth. The coops were placed on the fresh ground, and the ducklings would be hatched under the broodies. That was the plan. By that first spring, a motley assortment of what we believed to be 'small chickens' were in residence, but none of them were to prove of the slightest use. I had put my breeding programme together far too late in the day.

I collected the egg which the duck would lay every day and substitute a dummy in the nest; there would be ten or twelve before a clutch was complete. The duck would depart her chosen nest site to wash and feed at regular intervals; I learned the tell-tale signs from watching their patient and unobtrusive mates. Of course, I could not hear the intimate chatter of each drake and duck from my vantage point, but I have, over recent springs, come to recognise that of the wild shelduck.

For hour after hour I write the text of *Face to Face,* whilst overlooking Halspill Creek. Here, during May, drake shelduck idle on the edge of the tide. Suddenly, with loud staccato calls, an individual wheels away with rapid and purposeful flight across the estuary to land in the adjoining flood meadows. Simultaneously, a female, his

In June, a crèche of some twenty shelducklings will scamper across the bare mud of the tidal river Torridge, under the watchful eye of a couple of mothers.

female, appears from dense cover, probably from a rabbit burrow whose entrance is always above the level of the highest spring tides. Moments later, he is closely escorting her to her favoured feeding place. She stays for perhaps half an hour, no more; then after much audible conversation, they depart together to the vicinity of her nest.

I first witnessed this routine over fifty years ago on Portbury Wharf, close to the Severn Estuary. It is reassuring to know that much of our wild nature's long evolved routines still continue unchanged. Every year in early summer, in this first decade of the 21st century, shelducks follow the same behavioural patterns as here on the Torridge river, so close to my home. Maybe they are residents of the Cleddau estuaries in Pembrokeshire, or birds lost amongst the multitude of creeks on the north Norfolk coast, or finally, perhaps they are northern cousins favouring the salt marshes of the Solway Firth. Near our home, every June, a crèche of up to twenty ducklings, youngsters from several broods and under the watchful eye of a couple of mothers, scamper across the bare mud.

I would turn the collected eggs daily; I stored them in shallow trays on a bed of fine woodshavings. I would wipe the eggs with a wet cloth and keep the shavings slightly damp in an attempt to recreate the impact of a wild duck's wet plumage whenever she returns from a break. The membranes in the egg-shell stay soft in the damp vegetation of a nest site and ducklings hatch using a soft beak and egg-tooth to break out of the shell. This was crucial attention to detail in the years before complex incubators, which are the essential accessory for waterfowl enthusiasts today. Finally, the clutch would be set under a broody; nevertheless, I would still continue the daily egg-dampening routine.

It seemed an answer to my prayers when Dad returned with a broody hen. In no time, I had her on a clutch of eggs and left alone. However, I was trusting in lady luck. Early next morning all I could find was broken eggshells and dissipated yolks. Upset both by the journey and her sudden change in surroundings, the hen had trampled the clutch of precious Carolina eggs; she had never been fully broody and ready to sit tight; in any case, she was far too heavy a bird. Other hens arrived; a couple of red-crested pochard eggs started to chip, but none hatched with most of the ducklings 'dead-in-shell'. I was almost there, but these first attempts were proving disastrous and very frustrating.

There were, inevitably, family arguments over the lack of success. Dad was at his wits end to know where to search next for bantams and Mum had questioned more than once, and in no uncertain terms, about the futility of keeping the birds, having fertile clutches of eggs and, then, failing to hatch and rear any youngsters. "Pointless, completely pointless," Mum would argue, telling Dad and I to "get your act together".

The summer term, playing cricket, sped by and I devoted the autumn term to my first passion, rugby. Christmas and the New Year came and went; nevertheless, although adding two or three smaller hens to the flock, we had still failed to locate any bantams. Our farmer friend had explained that hens become broody when they have virtually completed their egg-laying cycle.

A most striking male red-crested pochard, *Netta rufina,* was the first individual in my collection in Clifton, Bristol, in 1956.
© John Peacham, North Devon, 2006.

So, it was vital to bring our birds into that condition as early as possible in the season.

"Give them plenty of protein," was his advice. So, for example, we allowed unused milk to turn off, to become 'lumpy and cheesy'. The hens would argue over every last slither. Every bird began to lay daily; I had to give their eggs away. The office staff, friends and neighbours had never eaten so many boiled eggs or omelettes!

A couple of hens went broody very early in the spring. Were we getting something right at last? Now, we needed the ducks to lay, and they did. However, if we thought we were on our way to immediate success, we were mistaken. Our lighter hens duly hatched their clutches with only the occasional dead-in-shell duckling or infertile egg; seven red-crested pochard, nine carolina and three common pintail, a species laying for the first time.

Now, the problem was to persuade the ducklings to settle and eat. I found achieving that was well nigh impossible. The ducklings were probably never really warm. I was giving them too much access to shallow water in my efforts to provide everything I thought they might need. The ducklings were constantly wet, never thoroughly dry and thus caught a chill. They were never really happy, and I can clearly remember them squeaking, constantly and plaintively. The Carolinas never stopped jumping and so exhausted themselves. I lost them all and the pintails too; but two young female pochards feathered beautifully. They joined a striking male which had been the first bird in my collection, boosting his prestige on the ponds alongside the other established breeding pair.

I now know that the Carolinas were jumping towards the light; they were mimicking something that happens naturally in the wild. The duck nests in holes in trees, sometimes sixty feet high in the forests of northern Canada. The newly hatched ducklings parachute from the nest entrance, landing softly on a carpet of pine-needles, before being led to the safety of the nearest water by the waiting parent. My ducklings just kept jumping, so exhausting themselves.

A decade later on an early summer's evening, I stood alongside Philip Wayre on the duck-rearing lawn at Hawks Hill, near Great Witchingham, his north Norfolk home. Around us were some twenty-five coops and runs full of young ducklings and goslings.

"Stand here for a few moments of an evening before you go home to your lodgings," he said, "and listen very carefully. Listen out for what will sound like distressed squeaking. Find out where it's coming from, and then do something about it. At least, come and tell me for a start. Remember, a squeaking duckling is a hungry duckling and a hungry duckling is a dead duckling." He was spot on!

Then suddenly, and it was now mid-June, came another surprise 'out of the blue'. During my frequent bird-watching trips to see the growing flocks of wildfowl gathering on the newly created Chew Valley Lake south of Bristol, I had forged a friendship with a maintenance worker. I would tell him about my waterfowl and he kept me informed of new species settling. Tufted ducks, particularly, favoured the water meadows adjacent to the lake, but the essential grass cutting and hedging would disturb the females on their nest sites. He said, "if ever ..., " then he would ring. By mid-summer, I had forgotten his words. The unexpected phone call found us rushing to his Bishop Sutton home to collect not one, but two, clutches. I still had one 'well-set' broody so kept one clutch; we took the other to my friend, Tommy Johnstone, curator of the Slimbridge collection.

Three attractive, chocolate brown youngsters hatched from eight olive green eggs, but as before, I encountered similar problems with the ducklings. However, one female was reared, and became exceptionally tame. She was an absolute delight for all who watched her; she would spend hours diving repeatedly in the deep pond in front of the offices retrieving the sunken grains of whole wheat, before suddenly reappearing 'bobbing like a cork' on the surface.

There was, too, another unexpected success that second summer. My female barnacle goose laid her first clutch. Both birds were outstanding parents, continually hostile to any other creature, human or otherwise, that ventured close to their territory. Three goslings were reared out of a clutch of four eggs. There were small dishes of water topped up with duckweed collected from the ponds in the nearby Ashton Park Estate. I scattered porridge oats on the weed and the silver-grey goslings, along with the young female Tufted, would eagerly devour the contents. It was strange how the barnacle parents only tolerated the Tufted to join their family; nevertheless, it was the Tufted youngster that had stimulated the goslings to feed well.

Had I stumbled, unwittingly, on a significant secret to rearing young waterfowl?

I still remember with affection the 'duck lawn' in north Norfolk. During my first summer one hundred and twelve barrow's goldeneye eggs, imported by air

The author with Tommy Johnstone, a friend and curator of the Wildfowl Trust's collection at Slimbridge, at the opening of the Wildlife Park in June 1967

© Jim Hale, 1967; courtesy Mia Hale

from Lake Myvatn in central Iceland, hatched from the ten dozen originally air-freighted by Willie Palsson. Unbelievably, one hundred and eight were reared, a staggering rate of success and unprecedented at the time; remember this was the summer of 1961!

Firstly, the youngsters were kept really warm by the innovative placement of an electric hot-plate screwed into the roof of each coop. Secondly, on every dish of pheasant starter crumb we placed a small pile of finely chopped hard-boiled egg, yolk only, along with a few maggots. Each brood was fed three times daily.

However, most importantly, a couple of mallard ducklings were introduced to each clutch of barrow's goldeneye as they hatched. The mallards would show no fear and would quickly settle, straight-away feeding well . Then, the goldeneyes would promptly copy them. Hadn't my Tufted played a similarly significant role?

I was also unaware, too, of how later that year, the barnacle gander gosling was to prove to be a very significant bird.

From time to time my father was requested to survey building sites well away from Bristol. Preliminary surveying preceded the drawing of the sketch plans, which would then be presented to the clients for their comments. Inevitably, I remember, the design Dad favoured was rarely chosen, much to his frustration! Eventually, a detailed

... we stopped on the bridge over the Teifi ... within moments I was focused on wigeon, *Anas penelope*, redwing, *Turdus iliacus*, and fieldfare, *Turdus pilaris* ...

application would be made to the local planning authority and work-ing drawings would be completed for the builders. Several on-site visits were necessary to ensure a successful conclusion.

"How do you fancy a trip to North Wales, not far from Snowdonia?" was Dad's opening remark at supper one evening. "The Filers," and John Filer was a Bristol builder with whom my father was much involved, "they've bought a derelict cottage very close to the Mawddach estuary. I'm sorry, I can't pronounce the name prop-erly! Anyway, I'm told the place is that close to the shore the lower ground level leads directly into a boathouse. The highest tides can flood inside over a cobbled floor."

"Sounds risky to me," interrupted Mum, "why do they go that far? Devon or Cornwall would be far more suitable; closer too!"

This was the mid-1950s. I now realise the Filer family were pioneers of a trend which has continued unabated ever since, particularly in the south west. Cottages are still purchased as second, or holiday homes, continually depriving young people of the chance to acquire affordable starter homes. The Filers loved north

European green-winged teal, *Anas crecca*, are one of my favourite wildfowl. I first enjoyed them at Chew Valley Lake and at Slimbridge in the early '50s. I still love their company and to hear the clear ringing whistles of the males during winter-time, just down the lane at Halspill Creek.
© Photolibrary Wales. www.photolibrarywales.com

Wales, with its hill walking and sailing; in fact, the estuary of the Mawddach with its backdrop of Cader Idris, and the proximity of the Irish Sea remains one of our most beautiful estuarine environments.

"I'll tell you what," continued Dad, "if we go across the Severn via the Aust Ferry and head through central Wales, we could go past that place where you said those geese winter. You know, you were telling me about them recently; something about they haven't long been officially recognised. Peter Scott and another chap persuaded some committee or other."

"You mean the Greenland Whitefronts? Yes, a flock does winter on the Tregaron Bog; and the other person was Christopher Dalgety."

"If we left early enough we would have an hour or so to explore, and see if there are any geese about. You never know. You must decide where we stay for two nights and work out the best route."

The trip was made immediately after the conclusion of the Christmas term, with Dad wanting his first drawings for the Filer family ready for them to study over the Christmas holiday.

We had decided to stay in Dolgellau, in the Royal Ship Hotel in Queen Square. With great anticipation, I had planned the route a dozen times and could name every town and village through which we would pass. We left well before first light, eating Mum's packed food on the road. My excitement grew as we came ever closer to the home of the wild geese. We had followed the Teifi valley north from Lampeter and approaching Tregaron, crossed the river for the first time. We turned left in the town, headed towards Aberystwyth and meeting the river again, we stopped on the bridge. We were then on the southern edge of the marshy wilderness and bog known today as Cors Caron. In front of us was the wide basin of the Teifi and beyond a still landscape stretching away to the western slopes of the Cambrian mountains, the river's source.

Within moments I was focusing my field glasses on mallard, wigeon, teal, curlew and lapwing. Flocks of chaffinches, linnets and goldfinches were foraging in the rough vegetation bordering the watercourses. They paused for no more than a few seconds before each hungry and chattering family group hurried on. Tiny redwings looked for rowan berries on the stunted bushes, whilst their larger cousins in the thrush family, the strikingly blue-grey fieldfares, probed the summer grazing meadows. These were now empty of stock, the local farmers would have removed the sheep, cattle and ponies two months previously. The Teifi was full and flowing fast, fed by innumerable streams from the surrounding hills. It was noticeably colder too, much colder than in Bristol.

"We'd best press on," advised Dad after a little while, "we've still a fair way to go and no doubt you'll want to stop again."

His words couldn't have been more prophetic.

We retraced our route back into town, before continuing north towards Pontrhydfendigaid. The bog reappeared, lying to the west now. The road skirted the Swansea to Aberystwyth railway line. We were slowing to take a sharpish left-hand bend when suddenly I was shouting, "Stop, we must stop."

I was out of the car before it was stationary. I was staring into a field that, quite literally, was full of bantams. There were bantams everywhere, along with a few much larger hens. Then I spotted a flock of mallard and next, well all I could blurt out to my father was, "a barnacle, there's a barnacle goose amongst all the bantams. Where do you think that's come from?"

"You'll never find out unless you ask," he replied pointing to a bungalow that lay back from the road.

A small, kindly-faced lady answered the door with, I assumed, her husband standing directly behind her. We had guessed correctly. They were responsible for the large flock of birds in the field. The lady first introduced herself as Elizabeth Owen and, in turn, her husband as Frank; he was a small, wiry man whom, I recall, had a distinct sharpness to the eye.

"Frank is keeper for the Estate and Bog. He also looks after the salmon fishing on the river here and for the Teifi Pools."

"And the bantams?" I enquired nervously.

Frank interrupted. "The bantams are kept for rearing the young pheasant poults and mallard ducklings. For the shooting."

"The barnacle goose?" I continued, my curiosity growing, "that's rather a stranger in the flock, isn't it?"

"Oh, that's Barney," replied Elizabeth, her soft blue eyes lighting up immediately. She continued in her soft, almost lyrical, Welsh accent. "She's my favourite, you see. She was wing-tipped by wildfowlers last winter on the Solway. They brought her down when they came for one of our shoots. They knew of Frank's waifs and strays and that I'd take special care of her. She's the only goose in the paddock and she really needs a mate. It's such a pity, you see."

I caught my father's eye as he gestured towards me and said, "David, tell Mr and Mrs Owen about your geese at home."

"I bred three young barnacles back in the summer. Would you like the young gander gosling as a companion for your bird?"

"A mate for my Barney, Christmas has come early. But we must give you something in exchange."

"I need silkie cross bantams to hatch and rear my ducklings." I said, rather bluntly. "We can't find any around Bristol and I've lost so many ducklings these past two summers."

"I could let you have a few," interrupted Frank. "Where did you say you were going? You could pick some birds up on the way home. In fact, I could have them boxed ready."

"And we could bring the gander with us on our next trip," added my father. "I'm bound to be coming back."

"If you could stay longer next time," continued Frank, "then I could take you out onto the Bog; we might see an otter. They live around here, you see, and I come across them regularly."

Otters! I couldn't believe what I was hearing.

I don't recall the rest of the journey after leaving the Owen's steading. Events had unfolded so dramatically that little was said. We were in a state of shock. I couldn't believe what we had just seen and what had been said in no more than ten minutes.

"Fifty bantams!" I said enthusiastically.

"More like a hundred," replied my father.

"Well a hundred then, plus a barnacle goose, maybe a chance to see an otter and bantams to collect on the way home. Wow!"

I do recall, however, the evening meal; it was jugged hare. I didn't know there was such a dish. Next day, the tumbledown building was, as Dad had described, tucked in close to the north shore of the Mawddach estuary, a mile or so upstream of Barmouth. On the sands at low water were the regulars I associated with such places. Shelduck, a few wigeon and teal, oyster catcher and curlew and several cormorants; there was always a couple diving in the tidal channel. The fishing must have been good. Many, standing motionless and looking almost prehistoric with wings outstretched, were clearly digesting their catch. Newcomers were ravens. During our surveying we saw and heard the same pair time and again as they crisscrossed the estuary with their February-born youngsters.

Downstream across the estuary's mouth was the railway bridge. However, my abiding memory is of Cader Idris, lying opposite and above Penmaenmawr. The mountain slopes, with the peak frequently drenched in the winter sun took on a different, but equally beautiful, hue every time I stopped to look. Stunning scenes would undoubtedly be enjoyed from the room Dad was planning as the first floor lounge; the purchase of this ruin was indeed far-sighted.

We stayed a second night in Dolgellau; this time supper was traditional Welsh mutton for supper; after an early breakfast we were on site for the final calculations. Nevertheless, it was already mid-afternoon before we had returned to the Owen's Maesllyn Cottage. Elizabeth insisted on us having tea; sliced bread and butter with home-made strawberry jam and sponge cakes, all served on the best china, of course. There was an even colder nip in the air than forty-eight hours previously as we loaded the bantams. Frank had chosen six pullets, their feathers a complex variety of beautiful colours. As we left, with me promising to write and to return with my young barnacle, a buzzard was circling lazily overhead. There were no red kites then. Now successfully re-established, the latter are integral to the present-day landscape of mid Wales.

"Shall we have one final look at the Bog?" Dad said suddenly as we entered Tregaron. "We're already far too late to make the last ferry at Beachley. Let's make best use of the remaining light and then take the alternative route home via Gloucester."

By the bridge where we had first stopped, both the river and the bog were eerily quiet as dusk approached, with just the occasional call in the far distance from a well-grown lamb still wanting the closeness of its mother. There were drake wigeon whistling close by, but we could not see them.

Suddenly, there was the call of geese.

"Where are they?" I called out, spinning around.

We had been looking into the vast wetland, the russet colours of the dying sedges reflecting in the last rays of sunlight. At first, the geese were silhouettes; then, in no time, they were overhead, still flying fast, but tumbling and dropping quickly. There was a gaggle of five; definitely an adult pair with their three youngsters. They landed out of sight to, spontaneously, more calls. So, other family groups

"Many cormorants were clearly digesting their catch; dunlin and turnstones were always busy."

© Peter Partington, 2006.
www.peterpartington.fsnet.co.uk

46

were already present at this evening roost. The wigeon sounded off again as these last arrivals separated some drakes from their mates. As wigeon do, they were taking umbrage at what they thought was an impolite disturbance.

Cors Caron is a very unusual place. It's something about the colour, rusty-red for much of the year. It's about the wildness of the place, of the big open skies above. It's the contrast with the green pasture and oak-wooded slopes on either side of the basin, which it dominates; welcome to the 'Red Bog'.
© and courtesy Jeremy Moore, www.wild-wales.com

There was no doubt the geese were Greenlands. Most would have been wintering on the Wexford Sloughs, but some had crossed the Irish Sea to the Dovey Estuary and this was yet another splinter group favouring the Bog's remote peatland pastures.

What a good call my father had made and what good fortune with which to conclude an extraordinary three days.

Greenland white-fronted geese assemble to breed in summer close to the west coast of, and adjacent to, the massive Greenland ice-cap south of Søndre Strømfjord. In 1979 and 1984, international expeditions had established that Iqaluit Nunavat held a high density of breeding geese. However, in 1988 a new breeding area, Naternaq, a vast area of flat, boggy plain close to sea-level and, unlike the rugged hill country of Iqaluit Nunavat, was mapped by aerial photography. The swampy landscape of Naternaq, with lakes full of suspended glacial sediments and therefore plant nutrients, is a wetland of massive proportions and is the summer home to possibly 6000 birds.

"It was noticeably colder too, much colder than in Bristol; the summer grazing meadows were now empty of their stock ... there were wigeon and teal ... and greenlands!"
© and courtesy Jeremy Moore, www.wild-wales.com

Dr Tony Fox, the world's leading expert on 'greenland numbers' then and today, and they are now rare as a world species, records how the

Danes, under Professor Fioras Salomonsen, had encouraged a major programme of ringing geese by the Greenlanders in the 1940s and '50s. The only bird recovered amongst the Welsh flocks was shot on Tregaron Bog. Greenlands migrate across the Northern Atlantic via Iceland to wintering grounds in the Inner and Outer Hebrides, in Ireland, and in north and mid-Wales. Did the female of the family group, which I saw late that December afternoon almost fifty years ago, lay her clutch of six eggs in a small depression amongst the Arctic tundra heath, also come from Ikamint, the small settlement amongst the archipelago of inlets and islands south of Brisko Bay?

My barnacle gosling duly went to Maesllyn, and I returned home on other occasions with yet more bantams. Nevertheless, I never did see an otter either on the marshes nor in one of the fresh water streams which meander across the lush water meadows.

I stayed in regular contact with the Owens over the years. Frank passed away, and Elizabeth moved, in her later years, into sheltered accommodation in Tregaron. We corresponded regularly, she always replying in the neatest of handwriting, especially given her age. Helen and I would take a very young Olivia to see her, and Olivia took to calling her 'Owens'; a couple of days around the Teifi valley and the Bog was, and still is, a 'must'. On the 19th November 2006, on my birthday, the three of us watched twenty goosander on Maesllyn Lake, not a stone's throw from the Owens's cottage.

I know our visits were highlights for her and brought back happy memories. We were always given tea, 'served on the best china,' of course! She loved to reminisce of the early days on the estate when she lived with Frank in the 'big house'. She recalled one very cold winter's night during the 1939-45 war when an old boar badger was allowed inside. He curled up in front of the log fire alongside the dogs and passed away. Frank had said that 'Brock' had returned to redeclare his family's birthright; nevertheless, its death had made a deep impression on Elizabeth.

Although increasingly immobile, she found great comfort in her deep faith. Her nurse read *Stormforce* to her and she enjoyed all the remarkable photographs of otters, those elusive creatures which she had enjoyed close to her home for most of her life. I felt privileged that she had allowed me to include two photos of Frank in the book.

Elizabeth Owen passed away peacefully, aged 94; I was the only English-speaking person at her funeral. The wake was held close to that bridge over the Teifi. I enjoyed traditional Welsh hospitality and found myself gazing at the very place where I first saw the family of five greenlands.

My lasting memory of her sparkling soul is intrinsically linked with this part of remote and wild Ceredigion.

Chapter Three

"David, don't just stand there, do something!"

European Eagle Owl; *Bubo bubo*
© John Threlfall 2007
www.johnthrelfall.co.uk

Owls of all species are regarded as symbols of wisdom. Perhaps this is because of their upright posture and their amazing eyes, which seem to look right through us; or perhaps it is because they look similar to us, as we are sure we are wise.

The Eagle Owl, Europe's largest owl and one of the biggest of all owl species is distributed over much of Europe and is now re-establishing itself throughout northern parts of the UK.

For most of its life it leads a solitary existence and although the male and female remain within the same territory, they hunt alone and roost separately. Males attract females by making very deep, far carrying booming calls commencing well before and continuing long after sunset. Once paired, they form a bond that lasts for life.

SHORT - EARED OWL,
(Asio flammeus.)

Of all the owls, the Short-eared is my favourite;
their buoyant and wavering flight, with wing-beats rowing
in slow-motion fashion; before gliding freely, are best seen
over open country. on Islay and Jura in high summer, or
over the Somerset Levels during the short winter days, as below

A telephone call to the Wildlife Park early one morning was from Dr John Sparks of the Bristol based BBC Natural History Unit. He had recently returned from north of the Arctic Circle. The camera team had been filming, under his astute direction, the great variety of creatures that congregate in the high latitudes of the circumpolar north, to take advantage of the almost continual daylight during the three months of the polar summer. As well as focusing on the migratory species, particularly the seabirds, wildfowl and waders, the team had also concentrated on the lives of three hunters who make their permanent home in these barren wastes. So, one of the goals had also been to capture sequences of polar bears, arctic foxes and snowy owls.

A review of the forthcoming television series had to be completed for *Radio Times* and John Sparks wanted to feature as the main illustration, a 'close-up' of a Snowy owl sitting on an outcrop of rock whilst clasping a lemming in its talons. If all went well the picture would double-up for the cover of the magazine's weekly edition. He had returned with some dead lemmings which had been kept frozen; the grapevine within the Unit had mentioned that I was hand-rearing a female Snowy owl in my Wildlife Park's collection just two or three miles away across Bristol.

"Aah, can you help?" was John's first question. "Might your 'snowy' stay still long enough with at least one foot on the prey for photos to be taken? And, aah, just one other detail; could we photograph the bird from below so that it would be silhouetted against the sky? That would be even better still!"

I was to get to know John Sparks well, and we have remained good friends. He has always been a perfectionist, always striving to have the shot or sequence absolutely correct, not only technically

adult male Snowy owl, *Nyctea scandiaca*

51

My female 'snowy' looking anxious; she coped well with the basics, but was always thrown by unforeseen events.

but exactly capturing the behaviour of the species in the wild. It was this work ethos in his directing and producing of films and in the compilation of his books, which explains his rise through the world-renowned NHU; he became the Head during 1983 in one of its most productive periods, when *Birdwatch, Reefwatch* and the acclaimed *Nature of Australia* were broadcast. He clearly held this esteemed post in his own inimitable style.

Mid-morning, a fortnight later, and we had correctly called a day with blue sky recapturing high summer in the Arctic. Sadly, although my owl had continued to 'tame' and in spite of many near misses, the snowy and I could not quite combine to achieve the required shot; there were just too many new circumstances for her to overcome simultaneously. I was disappointed to let the team down. However, although the snowy progressed, she proved to be a bird which only coped with the basics well, such as travelling and sitting still on the block or glove. Unfortunately, she was always thrown by unforeseen events.

John Sparks has written several highly regarded books; *Owls*, jointly with his friend Tony Soper, has been reprinted several times such has been its demand; *Realms of the Russian Bear* accompanied his television series of the same name; the latter was three years in the making over several time zones stretching across the roof of the world of the former USSR, from the Barents Sea in north-western Europe to the Bering Sea north of Kamchatka in the Far East.

However, I did succeed with my European eagle owl. I recall an episode from the television series *The Discovery of Animal Behaviour*, which was accompanied by Sparks' book of the same title.

I was to dress in the costume of a medieval rook-catcher and be filmed with 'Gonzo' in rural Dorset. Owls were used centuries ago to 'decoy' unsuspecting birds into being trapped or netted. Rook pie was considered a delicacy. I was to rendezvous very early one summer's morning at Hugh Miles' home. He was the cameraman and Sue, his wife, was to be my wardrobe and make-up artist.

The costume fitted well, but a problem had arisen because two right boots had been sent by the 'props' department in London. The shoot could not be postponed so I had no choice but to struggle on.

A long approach across ploughed fields to the copse location did not help; nevertheless, the owl behaved impeccably. After many tight shots in the pollarded undergrowth and although I was in some discomfort, the required sequences were steadily completed without any real difficulties.

It was very late in the traditional lunch hour when our small specialist team converged on the local pub. By then, there was little sitting room left. It was John's idea that I should be the person to find some space. He reckoned that with my uncouth appearance and blackened face and hands, along with the musty odour from clothes that clearly had spent most of their time in damp storage, I would clear an area. By the time the drinks had arrived and the food had been ordered, John had been proven right. Suddenly there was more than enough space for the whole team!

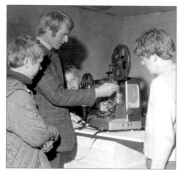

Dr John Sparks, Head of the BBC Natural History Unit, sharing his enthusiasm for the natural world with youngsters from my Junior Naturalists Club at the Wildlife Park

© Jim Hale, 1972, courtesy Mia Hale.

Wildlife stories with anecdotes and breaking news were shared; John Sparks and Hugh Miles, the latter affectionately known as 'Huge Smiles', were then, and still are, two great naturalists and lovers of the wild natural world. Their impact and influence on wildlife film making and programme production, have helped us to secure a greater understanding of vital conservation issues worldwide. As I have acknowledged some of John Sparks' productions, I now recognise some of Hugh Miles' achievements, *Flight of the Condor, On the Tracks of the Wild Otter* and *Kingdom of the Ice Bear*, a co-production with Mike Salisbury, an outstanding contemporary within the Unit. Inevitably, comments such as 'of enduring significance' are prompted from their peers and critics.

The telephone call was from a researcher from Animal Magic, the long-running and renowned children's wildlife programme which was televised 'live' from the Bristol studios each week. Could I bring the 'snowy' for an interview with Johnny Morris? I was aware of the programme's format because I had already contributed my first presentation.

On Boxing Day 1966, I had collected my first wild otter cub from Salthouse on the Norfolk marshes, near Cley-next-the-Sea. Bob Cooke, an auxiliary coastguard, had put his English springer spaniel Judy out onto the wet mud of an ebbing tide to fetch the stranded cub. He told me that, once home, it was vital to find a source of eels. At that moment, I was with him on the marshes immediately opposite his home; he was struggling to drag a sodden but tight bundle of straw from the cold murky waters of a drainage ditch before 'peeling' off a half-bucketful of clinging, or half-buried, slippery silver eels of varying sizes.

My research took me to a 'fish house' at Epney on the River Severn near Gloucester. Tons of elvers netted by fishermen from the bank whilst running up-river in early spring, were brought there and along with home-smoked full-grown eels and 'jellied' eels, were then sent to London's Billingsgate fish market. They were exported, too; the elvers were destined for release into rivers, particularly in Poland, but also throughout northern Europe. Every time I visited I discovered more about the mysterious life cycle of eels.

I wrote to George Inger, the programme's producer, suggesting I might tell the eels' story. In due course, I was filmed at Epney and, subsequently, I dubbed my commentary over the film. On transmission there were live eels in a tank, the edited film clip and an interview with Johnny Morris. A screen was progressively lit illustrating the elvers 5000 kilometre migratory journey as they followed the North Atlantic Drift or Gulf Stream.

Tiny larva, blade-like and almost transparent, born at moderate depth in the Sargasso Sea, drift in their countless millions to reach our rivers after three years. They are then elvers, eel-like in shape. In ditches and ponds they mature and between nine and fifteen years of age they embark on a return journey back to the Sargasso to breed and then die. How, over countless centuries, do the elvers know to which river to return? A mature eel from the Severn returns to the ocean in a south-westerly direction; an eel descending the Humber has to make its way either initially through the North Sea or turn south towards the English Channel before completing the ocean crossing. How do the eels' offspring, drifting at the mercy of the ocean currents, know to which river to return to continue their incredible life's cycle? I remember saying to Johnny Morris in that interview, "This is still an Animal *Mystery*, and one of many, too."

I found the story then astonishing, and we still do not know the answers today. I submitted another 'Magic' or 'Mystery' story about gannets and their island home of Grassholm, lying off west Wales. After daily fishing trips, how do the male birds instinctively find their way home to their partner, lost amongst a sea of thousands of white dots? I entitled the item 'Seabird City'. I never received a reply which has tarnished my image of what I thought the programme was setting out to achieve. Maybe 'they' were quite happy with just providing images from the studio, along with easily obtained film from the wild, as technology continued to progressively improve. I do not think that, even today, some wildlife presenters have the humility to admit that we still do not understand enough about the complexities of the highly evolved natural world; that is probably because they are first and foremost 'media' presenters, and not naturalists.

My vehicle, a Bedford Commer one-ton van, had been allocated a space in the scene dock giving quick access to and from the recording studio. All went to plan. There were other live exhibits; tame parrots and macaws had been brought by Betty Risdon who, with her husband Donald, had established the Tropical Bird Gardens at Rode near Bath. Betty was a regular contributor. Her birds, displayed on stands at different heights, gave Johnny the opportunity to conduct impromptu off-the-cuff 'conversations' with each individual. The cameras would capture at very close quarters the puzzled expressions of the birds as they gently cavorted, somersaulted and sidled towards him on their perches. Johnny was a past-master in

Snowy owls on their breeding territory within the Pjorsa Oasis in central Iceland; females stagger their egg-laying to ensure older chicks will survive during periods of food shortage, when the latter will also eat their younger, weaker siblings.

© Peter Partington 2007. www.peterpartington.fsnet.co.uk

producing contrasting voices and aided by well-scripted texts, he created fun and true-to-life dialogues, all 'must-watch' television in those days for youngsters nationwide.

Johnny Morris's ability was that he could rapidly improvise on the bare bones of a storyline, and still come to the same planned conclusion. Gerald Durrell, as I shall record elsewhere, was another similarly gifted individual, although his rare talent was more associated with his deep knowledge of species in the wild, the lemurs of his beloved Madagascar immediately spring to mind. Nevertheless, it was Morris's vivid imagination, the ability to coin a phrase in an instant, the intonations and varieties of voice, whilst simultaneously contorting his face to match the voice, which gave him an unrivalled ability in the studio. How greatly he engaged and enthused young people's minds for over two decades has never been fully recognised. Animal Magic was prematurely axed, but was followed by other children's wildlife series such as Tony Soper's Wildwatch and The Really Wild Show. Nevertheless, for youngsters of primary school age, there is still the need for an 'Animal Magic' format and a 'Johnny Morris' presenter to give them their first formative insights into the magical beauty and joys of wild nature found on Planet Earth.

The day had slipped quickly by and soon it was time to briefly attend make-up. In the studio, the programme had been rehearsed 'from the top' twice; with one or two 'sticky' passages more often than that. All the participants waited apprehensively.

"And now it's time to cross to Bristol for this week's edition of Animal Magic, presented by Johnny Morris," came the announcer's calm voice from London. That was immediately followed by the ever-familiar and never to be forgotten title track over the opening titles and graphics. How many readers will fondly remember their weekly date with Animal Magic and will still be able to instantly hum the theme music. The time for my interview was close.

I discussed the more matter-of-fact information; that snowies live circumpolar but only in the Arctic north with no similar species filling the same niche in Antarctica; that their favourite food was lemmings and the young of wildfowl and waders which breed on their large hunting territories; I gave further details about my bird; that she was a young female, then some fifteen months of age, but parent-reared. I was handling her regularly so she could join my lecture 'squad'. However, I particularly wanted to stress data that reflected for me the essential ethos of the programme and which was mirrored in its title. I worked into the conversation the remarkable ability that snowies have of foretelling the availability of their main food source in the short summer weeks. Unpredictable and as yet unknown factors mean litters of lemmings will either explode, remain average or in some years even fail.

How do female snowies know whether to lay a clutch of up to nine eggs in the knowledge that around the time the eggs hatch their food source will be in abundance? Or, conversely, how do they know after courtship and mating that they should lay only two or three eggs and maybe even none at all; then five or six weeks later, that same food source has crashed dramatically for some inexplicable reason.

I recall now that most of what I planned to say was included. I hope it not only made sense but reinforced a key aspect which I still stress in my presentations today, particularly to Year 6 youngsters in community junior schools. No matter how many books have been written or television series have been made, and although our knowledge of the natural world has greatly increased over the forty years since that 'snowy' interview, we are still only scratching the surface of what we know and understand about creatures and environments. Their sublime magic is still there for us to grasp and embrace. Nevertheless, over the same period, we have brought untold pressure on both. In addition we have, and continue to, exploit and abuse the resources on which they, and ultimately we, will depend for survival.

Meanwhile in the studio, the remainder of the programme ran its course. This included Johnny putting a dialogue over pre-recorded film of him dressed as a keeper, chatting to and feeding sealions and penguins. I had to walk unobtrusively across the studio to a pre-planned spot marked with a taped white cross. As the final moments drew to a close, two cameras withdrew from Johnny and were pushed to take up position in front of, but just either side of me, as I held the snowy owl.

The plan was to increasingly close in on the face of the owl, producing an ever larger image, during the forty seconds or so of the closing titles sequence. The monitor set at my feet was showing the pictures on the television screens in homes across the nation; they were being selected by the vision mixer in the production room above the studio from one of the two cameras at which the owl continued to stare. The end caption would read "BBC Colour, Bristol" with the year in Roman numerals beneath, and during the final seconds the plan was to have just the eyes of the owl filling the screen. It had worked successfully in rehearsal, twice!

Johnny wrapped the broadcast by saying, "see you all again next week, so bye bye for now," and I heard the signature tune.

After some twenty seconds a bank of spotlights suddenly blew out directly above me. There were other banks of spotlights; there was no reduction in the intensity of light, there was only a brief sound similar to a strip light failing. In the studio, only I and the crew in the immediate vicinity heard anything as, of course, did the owl. She remained still but instantly tightened her grip, and I mean *really* tightened her grip. My left hand was in a vice! She had sunk her talons into my flesh, easily puncturing the glove; and the glove was the one I always used when handling my golden eagles!

The transmission was live to a young audience, and standing right in front of me, the floor manager immediately put one finger to his lips, clearly indicating he wanted no sound. Although I was aware that no one could see my expression there was anguish on my contorted face. I was almost standing on one leg, such was the pain. It seemed an absolute age before he raised both hands with ten fingers displayed. Then, there was just the one hand showing five, but recalling events now, I am sure those final five seconds became ten as he erred on the side of caution, before finally calling "cut" with a brief horizontal movement of one hand.

I would prefer to remember that my expletives were fairly mild, nothing more perhaps than "bloody hell". Nevertheless, the grip was still vice-like and the pain severe. The problem was that the snowy would not jump to the sanctuary of her block as I expected. I was unable to prise any individual talon out of my flesh so it was also impossible to remove the glove.

I was approached by the studio nurse and I explained that I would report to her just as soon as the owl had released her grip. Meanwhile, the stage crew continued to dismantle the set. I retreated to the cool atmosphere and solitude of the scene dock and 'misted' the bird, but all to no avail. I went outside into the BBC grounds and, eventually, walked down Tyndalls Park Road to the traffic lights, turned and walked up Whiteladies Road towards the main entrance of the BBC West of England TV Centre.

At half past five, I was sitting on a garden wall opposite the then Territorial Army Barracks as dozens of pedestrians hurried past in the darkness on their way home. The snowy was rather bizarrely lit by the orange street lighting and many passers-by suddenly took a second look with startled expressions. Was that large white owl they had just seen really alive?

Well over an hour later in the now-deserted scene dock, the owl, for no apparent reason, suddenly released her grip. She immediately sprang to her block. I 'misted' her for the umpteenth time, knelt close to her, tethered her and she promptly started to preen as if she hadn't a care in the world.

The nurse cleaned my sore hand. A day later it was very swollen with bruising tinged red, blue and purple. The hand felt as if it had been slammed in a car door.

When snowies catch their prey, it is the hind claw or talon that undoubtedly locks onto the prey. I knew then and have been reminded several times since that ounce for ounce, pound for pound owls, all owls, whatever their age, have a far stronger grip than corresponding day-time hunters.

Foolish but unintentional mistakes, made whilst working with Philip and Patricia Wayre, often nearly resulted in me being sacked and sent home. One classic occasion concerned their pair of snowy owls.

During the summer months, guests were invited by the Wayres to stay over a weekend at their Hawks Hill farmhouse set amidst the rolling countryside of north Norfolk. They would be friends or associates from the world of natural history coming to enjoy, at close quarters, the rapidly growing wildlife collection, to discuss the latest news and their plans for breeding rare and endangered species. Several 'firsts' for a UK collection had already been achieved.

Visitors arrived at the farm late on Friday afternoons either directly by car, or having been collected from Norwich Thorpe

Station. After tea and before the evening meal, to which the Wayres always generously invited me, Mr Wayre would escort their guests around part of the collection and I would accompany him.

I was there, for example, to gently flush out a particular pair of pheasants from thick cover which the birds both needed and favoured and which was so necessary for their successful nesting. Mr Wayre was rightfully very proud of his achievements with all three species of Tragopans; Cabot, Satyr and Temmincks. There were very few other individuals, the cock birds are the most striking and richly plumaged of all the pheasants, in any other collections worldwide in the early 1960s.

I would delay the afternoon feed for the waterfowl ponds close to the farmhouse; the birds would therefore be keener and come much closer to hand. The scattering of whole wheat would bring the flocks of geese rushing back from across their grazing paddocks, to where they had dispersed since early morning, to be hand-fed .

There were breeding family groups of many species; busy, inquisitive and endearing Emperor geese from Alaska were kept alongside the taller and rather haughty Barheaded geese from the Indian sub-continent. From the northern Arctic regions, redbreasted, barnacle, dark-bellied Brents, Ross's and Lesser snow geese, were a

"Ravens' deep 'cronking' calls are strangely comforting; ... I feel a need to hear them daily."

chattering, gossiping, almost prattling flock which, nevertheless, were very compatible; this was a disposition which encouraged many of them to nest alongside one another.

East Anglia was and still is a mecca for private wildfowl collections; in the early '60s, four names were already to the fore; Jack Williams and Bill Perowne were, respectively at Tunsted and South Creake, in Norfolk; Oliver Squire's birds were near St Neots, in Cambridgeshire. The early and tragic loss of Rodney Dawson, who farmed in Lincolnshire, and subsequently on Islay in the Inner

Hebrides, robbed the wildfowl world of a genius with seaducks and sawbills. The best collection, founded by Bill Makins, is open these days to the general public, and is to be found at Pensthorpe, near Fakenham. Nevertheless, in '61, Mr Wayre's collection was already comprehensive; the birds were in fine health, proof being in the very high number of fertile clutches of eggs regularly being laid.

I had been informed that two middle-aged ladies were coming to stay. I forget now who they were and their standing in the world of natural history at that time. I was given the details of the itinerary at the Friday morning breakfast 'briefing' at which Mr Wayre had also indicated that he wanted, on this occasion, to include the ravens, the European eagle owls and the snowy owls as well as the usual wildfowl ponds in the introductory walk. So would I make ready half a bucket of dead chicks as well. He planned for me to enter the flights to hand feed the birds.

At seven o'clock in the morning, just after my arrival on the farm, I would feed the young ducklings and pheasant chicks. Immediately after breakfast, my next routine was to kill the required daily quota of young chickens. I found that an unpleasant and distressing procedure especially coming from a previously urban environment. Nowadays, day-old cockerels, distinguishable at birth from pullet chicks by a distinctive variation in colour, are humanely gassed in their tens of thousands just after hatching. They form part of a substitute diet, with multi-vitamin supplements added, for birds of prey and carnivores, in private and public zoological collections.

Today, they can be bought blast frozen, in boxes of '250' or by the '1000', they can be stockpiled, stored in freezers with the requisite daily number being thawed overnight. It is 21st century unit catering! In 1961 in Norfolk the young day-olds were brought in from one of a burgeoning rash of hatcheries that were emerging in eastern England. We were witnessing the beginnings of the fast food industry when chicken became the first affordable 'eat-out' meal for millions of people. In my home city of Bristol, Berni Inns were synonymous with that social phenomenon. Kentucky, Little Chef, MacDonalds and Burger King are now the household names.

At Hawks Hill, the chicks were fed until required; towards the end of our stock another five hundred or a thousand birds would be forwarded. I had been shown the most humane and efficient way to dispatch a youngster; I had to exert downward pressure from my thumb onto the neck over a sharp ridge. Sensitive to this method of ending a little creature's life, I had quickly fallen into the slack habit of holding the chick with its legs between the first two fingers of the hand, before quickly delivering a sharp blow to the back of the head.

Some time early that morning I must have lost concentration as some thirty to forty birds were made ready. Unfortunately, I only stunned one individual leaving it, unknowingly, unconscious. Several hours later it had revived; nevertheless, it lay trapped under its lifeless companions in the bucket.

I was alongside Mr Wayre and his two lady guests as we approached the aviaries with all having previously gone well. The waterfowl had gathered closely around according to plan, although the geese had grumbled at their later feed-time. I had briefly handled the golden eagle and the European eagle owl on the glove in their respective mews and both ladies had been suitably impressed. Mr Wayre had explained that I would be showing them the young ducks and pheasants on both rearing lawns the next morning.

Mr Wayre chose the ravens to be fed first. He had reckoned that their continuous calls, given the lateness of their feed, would prove a distraction to the owls. I had prepared scraps of rabbit and pheasant, originally road casualties, and sorted from the previous day's leftovers. Their main feed was a mix of rolled oats, minced carrot, maize, some fruit and sundry kitchen scraps from the farmhouse. The contents of this bowl reflected that in the wild, although predominantly feeders on carrion, the adult birds are also not averse to helping themselves to a range of alternative fare. These days, ravens, highly evolved, alert and quick to learn, are more than holding their own in western parts, and are extending their range eastwards; there is, no doubt, that they have benefited by being flexible and accommodating feeders in difficult times. Unseen by our pair, I had previously left their food dishes outside the back door of the enclosure. The plan was simple. As I entered I would throw a couple of chicks towards the front of the pen; the ravens would immediately pounce on them. They would then be in front of the guests who would appreciate their striking features; the adult birds sport a metallic blue-green sheen to their feathers. Next, I would introduce the two bowls of food, adding only at the very last moment a couple of infertile duck or pheasant eggs, their daily treat.

As soon as I retreated the ravens immediately collected the eggs before hopping away to bury them. They both went to great lengths to use the long grass, always purposely left uncut, to complete the stashing away of their booty, with each individual trying their utmost to prevent the other from detecting the whereabouts of their spoils. When trying to bury or cover the egg, each bird would clearly present its back to the other, a routine completed every time they were given an egg. So there was no problem with the birds showing off their uncanny and sly routines, even with strangers close by. Of course, Mr Wayre could explain that the birds were, in fact, simply following the typical behaviour of all corvids. The ravens' wild cousins similarly follow these traits in whatever wild country is their home. Over forty years later, I regularly watch and hear our resident family in

female Snowy Owl,
Nyctea scandiaca
"... she would immediately weave and
bob her head in anticipation ..."
© John and Tracy Langley, Chester
www.ourwildlifephotography.co.uk

'the Land of the Two Rivers'. Although traditionally thought of as birds of foreboding, their deep 'cronking' calls are strangely comforting, especially in bleak wintertime. I feel a need to hear them daily.

Next, it was the turn of the snowy owls. In this aviary, it was always the larger female bird which instantly acknowledged me. She would call gently and affectionately as I entered, weaving and bobbing her head in anticipation of my next predictable move. In contrast, the male was quite nervous, remaining absolutely still on his perch and staring directly ahead. He was especially immobile if suddenly aware that more than one person or strangers were about. This would happen, only during summertime and then about once a fortnight; he was comfortable only when being fed by one individual or when Mr Wayre was making his regular evening tour of the grounds, accompanied by his two pointer bitches, Whisper and Pippykin. However, the dogs were never that close to the enclosure and Mr Wayre would, on most occasions, be walking briskly past.

I knew it was important to enter the pen and slip past the male on his high perch as quietly and quickly as possible, preventing his sudden take-off and crash into the wire netting. I was still concentrating on his possible reaction as I put my hand into the bucket to lob the first chick for the female. As I let it go, I felt a slight movement in my hand. However, I had actually thrown the little bundle before the sensation of movement and its significance had engaged with my brain!

Everything was now happening as if in slow motion in front of the watching audience. On landing in the long grass, the chick cheeped as young chicks do. I looked at Mr Wayre, and for once he was speechless. Both ladies gazed at the chick. I looked across to the snowies. The male was completely unaware of the situation, but not so the female. She was well alert, rotating her head even

female Eagle Owl, *Bubo bubo*.
Gonzo's filming for an episode of the
'Discovery of Animal Behaviour' series
was the first of many successes
© John and Tracy Langley, Chester
www.ourwildlifephotography.co.uk

more enthusiastically than usual. Suddenly, the female launched herself towards the front of the pen and dropped directly onto the spot where I had last seen the hapless chick.

"David, don't just stand there, do something." I heard Mr Wayre say in a strangely controlled way. Surprisingly, there were none of his usual accompanying barrage of expletives.

The female was motionless, staring at her feet, and I feared the worst. However, moments later, and I couldn't believe my luck, nor for that matter the chick's good fortune, there it was scampering back towards me. Fortunately for both of us the male bird was still unaware that part of his supper was rushing towards him. I quickly came to my senses and grabbed the little blighter, popped him into the bucket and retreated very calmly, and with composure I may add, out of the aviary.

"I'll see you back at the farm," were Mr Wayre's stern last words as he strode away with his guests. Come to think of it both the snowies and the still waiting and expectant eagle owls went without their food that evening.

"... David - don't just stand there -
DO SOMETHING!"

A while later, I entered the farmhouse kitchen. I didn't know whether I was still going to join everybody for supper or whether I would be told, literally, to 'get on my bike'.

"I gather you managed to suitably entertain our guests," Mrs Wayre chuckled, with a twinkle in her eye. Patricia had a wicked sense of humour.

"Am I staying for...?" I stumbled feebly.

"Don't be silly, of course you are," she interrupted, "forget the whole episode. I gather Philip thought it was hilarious. He said it stunned the two old dears into complete silence."

Nothing further was said during supper about the incident. In fact, the conversation ranged over many wildlife issues of the time, and how the ladies were planning to travel the next day, the Saturday, to Blakeney quay. From there they were to take one of the 'Bean family' boats to Blakeney Point. They had permits to land and to photograph the tern and common seal colonies. Forty-five years later, visitors to the 'Point' still photograph common seals and their pups in mid-summer. Nowadays, in the late autumn and around Christmas-time, grey seals are there with their calves, too; and you still make that special trip on a 'Bean' boat.

Early next morning, it was my turn to escort the ladies around my favourite part of the collection, the duck and pheasant rearing lawns. They were most attentive and courteous, Eventually, it was time to take my leave and as I wished them a good day on the coast one of them turned to me and said, "I say, that was rather exciting with that dear little chick and the female Snowy last evening. Does she ever catch them?"

I was flabbergasted.

"We never feed live food," I explained firmly, "that was a complete mistake on my part."

"Well anyway, bye for now," the one continued. She hadn't taken in a word that I had said, "We look forward to catching up with you when we get back tonight for some more fun and games."

To this day I am not sure whether they believed me. I remember being determined to encounter them again if only to explain that I had taken the unfortunate chick back to my lodgings at the Bell Inn in Bawdeswell. It deserved that second chance. The pub's licensees, Mr and Mrs Walter Larke, would surely know many smallholders, country dwellers with allotments and the like, who kept and hatched a few chickens and pheasants every year. There had to be someone who would take pity on and rear this chick so that it could run free and forage away from any more owls.

Wherever that might be, he or she would always be a chicken with a remarkable tale to recall to his or her companions!

Chapter Four

" 'Wildlife Face-to-Face.'
What do you think?"

Tawny Owl: *Strix aluco*
© John Threlfall 2007
www.johnthrelfall.co.uk

The tawny owl is the commonest owl of our deciduous woodlands.

When icicles hang by the wall,
And Dick, the shepherd, blows his nail
And Tom bears logs into the hall,
And milk comes frozen home in pail,
When blood is ripp'd and ways be foul,
Then nightly sings the staring owl;
Tu-who; Tu-whit, tu-who ....

Shakespeare
Love's Labour's Lost

Common Buzzard

much larger than the male kestrel which is near by & gives a super comparison.

Common KESTREL

This is a male & Shows an all g~ tai with a blac~ Terminal band

grey crow~ & nape

This Common Buzzard is very alert & hunting for Rabbits

Tawny Owl are double the size of Little Owl
a noticable line of White Tips to Scapulars.

LITTLE OWL

Little Owl are quite dark with strong white spots
Strong White eyebrows

Little Owl Show bold Yellow Iris's Compared to the all dark eye's of Tawny Owl

TAWNY OWL

'The Gang of Four', the author's lecture squad over many years

W omen's Institute (WI) Area Group Meetings, are inevitably memorable and fun occasions. As many as ten or twelve individual members can attend from up to half a dozen Institutes. Each WI takes it in turn to present the meeting which is held in the host's village community hall. Autumn and Spring gatherings are organised every year and, on this spring occasion, the venue for my presentation was Eardisley Village Hall, near Hereford.

I have long since learnt when illustrating with live exhibits, that it pays dividends to arrive in the area well beforehand. In fact, nowadays, through the organising secretary, I request an early access to the hall, often meeting with the caretaker at least a couple of hours in advance. Then, I can discover a couple of small quiet ante-rooms, where tethered hawks and owls can be held.

In the early 1980s my lecture 'squad' consisted of four birds of prey that would always be 'blocked' in front of an audience, these included a female buzzard, a male kestrel, a male tawny owl and a female little owl. In addition, I travelled with a couple of tame foxes and badgers which I could fetch from the vehicle with my accompanying member of staff. The most pressing requirement was a couple of rock-steady trestle tables, which I would position so that nobody could intrude into the area behind the birds. I had large, but portable, card-mounted and framed photographs of each species,

"The tubular form of owls' eyes has been evolved, presumably, to save space inside the skull; because of this, owls' eyes are not capable of rotary movements. Owls, however, make up for their fixed eyes by having exceptionally mobile necks; the head can rotate through at least 270 degrees" Clearly, it cannot pass through and beyond 360 degrees!
source: *Owls, their natural and unnatural history*,
John Sparks and Tony Soper, Appendix 1, 1979

which stood vertically behind each exhibit. In front, there was other information on each exhibit presented on laminated sheets; a small central table held personal information, including flyers and postcards, to be handed out on request, all of which completed an attractive and comprehensive display. The members of a group, their guests and other visitors could look closely at and enjoy the varied information at their leisure, both before and after my hour-long presentations.

That lovely spring April evening in rural Herefordshire was no exception to the usual format. I had met with the caretaker, found everything I had needed, and had introduced myself to the first arrivals of Eardisley WI's organising committee. They were the lady members who were responsible for preparing the customary gener-ous buffet supper and the tables on which, eventually, all the visit-ing groups competition entries would be displayed. These, as the guest speaker, I would later have to judge .

Now it was time for me to find the local public house and enjoy a pork pie, some crisps and a pint of Guinness. It was there that I planned to discover the names of a couple of local livestock farms and deciduous woodlands. I was following the advice of Gerry Belton, but more of Gerry's role in a moment. I would be able for just that one talk to remind the audience of local landmarks which, in turn, they would easily recognise. That knowledge, briefly offered, would also raise a question with the audience; how come the speak-er knows our area so well? So, a while later that night when I intro-duced the buzzard or the tawny owl, I would have said something for example along these lines about the owl:

"The tawny owl is the commonest owl of our woodlands, and it is roundabout now that some individuals, not that far from here, in such-and-such wood, (from a flash card I would have memorised its identity), are becoming active, waking from their daytime slumbers, stirring from their favourite roosting haunts, to begin hunting for their favourite prey..."

The landlord duly obliged with the locations and having also skimmed the local newspaper left on the bar for any other relevant and up-to-date news items or reports on local wildlife issues, such as the threat to a local badger sett from a new housing development, I made my way back to the hall.

There is no doubt that this attention to detail, certainly in terms of the setting-up of the live exhibits, was inspired by working alongside the naturalist Philip Wayre. I was on a steep learning curve all the time whenever and wherever I accompanied him as his 'pupil'. The latter was a term of endearment with which he used to introduce me when on assignments. I worked for him at Hawks Hill, his home near Great Witchingham in Norfolk, during most of 1961 and 1962, a long gap period before Cambridge University beckoned. As well as lecturing regularly, Mr Wayre was producing wildlife films; *Wind in the Reeds*, and *Wind on the Heath* were, at that time, his two projects for the recently formed ITV Anglia *Survival* Unit in Norwich. Then, and for many years afterwards, the term stuck; thirty years later, he was still referring to me as his 'erstwhile pupil'. This was in the introduction he wrote for a book called *A Travelling Otter*, penned by Ian Anderson and illustrated with beautiful line drawings by Ian's late wife, Gabrielle Bordewich. Gaby's drawings were completed from watching the British otters in my family group; at that time they were the only British otters licensed by English Nature, or the then Nature Conservancy Council, to a private individual in the United Kingdom.

However, finding out the names of nearby woodlands to 'localise' a talk with an audience was one of Gerry Belton's suggestions. He, at the time of our first meeting, was publicity officer for the Exmoor National Park Authority. It's headquarters were then, and still are today, at Exmoor House in Dulverton. Gerry knew of my successful lecture programme for schools which stayed during the Easter holidays at the Butlins Holiday Camp in nearby Minehead.

It was Paul Winterforde-Young and Diana Wall, later Diana Winterforde-Young, who had initiated my Butlins presentations. They realised my exceptionally tame exhibits were an unexpected opportunity to bring youngsters in close contact with creatures they might never see on the field outings planned for the nearby Quantock Hills and Exmoor. I would travel with my 'gang of four', plus my hand-reared tame foxes and badgers, up to three times a week, so popular were my talks. There was every chance that the youngsters would see wild hawks, but little prospect of then coming across owls. However, they would be shown the earths and setts where the wild families of fox and badger lived on the Quantocks.

On our first occasion together, Paul asked me to stand outside one of the large entertainment halls in which the Butlins 'Redcoats' entertained thousands of campers every evening.

"Stand there for a few minutes," he said, "and as people gather round, tell them about your buzzard; make her spread her wings as you demonstrated to me earlier. That was really impressive," he added, gesticulating with his arms. Within no time, thirty to forty people had gathered.

"That'll do," he interrupted a few minutes later, "that'll go down a bomb with the youngsters, particularly for those coming from our inner cities. They'll not have seen anything like that. Pop the bird back in your vehicle for now. You'll come and have some lunch with me?" he enquired.

Later, as we were finishing our meal, Paul took from his wallet a folded and well-thumbed Craven 'A' cigarette packet which

"...tell them about your buzzard; make her spread
her wings ... that was really impressive..."

both pictures © Ian Anderson, Somerset, 1982

he clearly treasured. There were a few lines drawn on the blank inside; this was the first rough sketch plan, outlined by Sir Billy Butlin, of the future camp site as visualised from the high hill that overlooks the town of Minehead. The marshy meadows lie only just above high water behind the shingle ridge which protects them from the highest tides of the Bristol Channel. They were destined to become one of Butlin's famous holiday camps, 'Butlins' Minehead, now known as Somerwest World. Paul told me that Sir Billy had given him less than eighteen months to bring his plans to fruition.

Paul was a great enthusiast and an encouragement to me all the time that I knew him. His sudden and early passing robbed very many people of a true and loyal friend.

Meanwhile, Gerry Belton had planned for me to present on three occasions during one August day for Exmoor's summer visitors; at Exford in the morning, in Porlock in the early afternoon and finally, wrapping the day, in Dulverton Town Hall. I had acquired a clue to his flair and organising ability during the several occasions he had telephoned to organise, check and then double-check the detailed itinerary. No one else had previously telephoned me so frequently prior to an event. Naturally, I am more apprehensive of occasions when I need to set up on more than one occasion and at different venues. However, I must admit that my fears were allayed on my arrival outside the Exford village hall early that August morning.

Gerry, it seemed, had every potential problem covered. Even before I had stopped the vehicle, he was

Whatever the time of year, we either see, or
hear, individual or family trios of buzzards
every day. For certain, they are part
of our landscape.

directing me into a specially designated parking space, right outside the front door. The cones had long been in position and the vehicle could not have been more adjacent. He was fully aware how its close proximity would ease the transfer of the live exhibits inside. There were similar arrangements in place in both Porlock and Dulverton.

Inside the hall he had, perhaps, gone a touch too far. He had watched one of my days at Butlins, so had set out the chairs in a circular fashion, intending for me to speak with the audience all around me. However, he had not realised that the birds needed to have at least one flank clear of any distraction, preferably the side behind them. In addition, curtains pulled across windows, were a bonus too. The elimination of activities outside a venue, such as the movement of people which creates threatening shapes and strange silhouettes for the birds, allows them to focus entirely on everything happening in front of them.

"...the tawny owl would, for no apparent reason, suddenly rotate his head through ninety degrees..."

© John Peacham, North Devon, 2006.

Nevertheless, a compromise was quickly reached. I reminded Gerry that each bird was to be removed from their respective block in turn and under gloved control and with the help of my staff, would be brought very close to the tightly packed audience. Nobody would miss out. It was in the next half hour that we both simultaneously thought of bringing all the youngsters together as one group into the front rows just before 'kick off'. Latecomers, through no fault of their own, now had a privileged and uninterrupted view. Now there was no need for them to be constantly on the move, standing up at the back and then being told by parents to sit down, all of which would disturb my birds. Now, no one would feel left out. It was a parent who had taken the wrong turning on the journey to the hall! I also wanted all the youngsters to enjoy the privilege of stroking and feeling the softness of the tawny owl's feathers; their shared involvement has always been paramount to my presentation's success.

"I've taken the liberty, too, of giving your talks a title," enthused Gerry excitedly; "and I've designed posters to match, I hope you don't mind. Come and have a look, they're displayed outside. I've used the photo of you with the buzzard." I was finding it hard to keep up with Gerry, such was his obvious commitment to the forthcoming day. "There you are, 'Wildlife Face-to-Face'. What do you think? The different times and venues are set out in the information panels.

They've been displayed for a while around each venue."

"That's kind of you. They're impressive, very eye-catching, and a new title for my talks, too!" I said, slightly taken aback.

"Now, we'll just have to sit back and see how many people will come. You see, that's been my challenge. This has been a new venture for the Park Authority. Now we're in the lap of the gods and the weather is going to be important, too." He paused. "Not too good tho', don't want beach weather today," he added with a smile moments later, as he hurried away to organise somebody else!

It was not long before the first visitors were occupying the front rows. Eventually all three venues were packed with many standing for the duration. The day was an unprecedented success for Gerry, the Exmoor National Park Authority and myself. I guess the reader will realise that subsequently, for some twenty-five years, my presentations with live exhibits have been entitled 'Wildlife, Face-to-Face'. It is no coincidence, too, that this book is called 'Face-to-Face with nature', as it truly reflects my lifetime's work and career. I shall always be indebted to Gerry for his creative flair and his accuracy of simply stating the obvious. He and his wife, Felicity, remain good friends to this day.

Now, many years later, and nearing seven thirty, the village hall in Eardisley was similarly becoming very full. I was waiting unobtrusively to one side. Few were aware of my presence; those who did notice me probably thought I was the caretaker, dressed as I was in one of my working smocks.

Groups of ladies were being ushered by their hosts into their allotted rows; it was clear from the various regalia and badges being worn that each Institute was represented by their respective President, Secretary and Treasurer with a bevy of other ladies completing each group. There were warm greetings as they recognised friends of many years standing from other nearby villages.

There was a regular pattern to their behaviour too. Each took off their coat and, in turn, folded it, put it under their chair but nevertheless, kept their handbag on their lap. Each then surveyed in their own time, the scene around them. There were tables brimming with wholesome home-prepared food, pies and quiches, sandwiches, scotch eggs, bowls of crisps and the usual variety of home-made cakes, the WI speciality. There was the host WI's main table complete with its resplendent themed and embroidered table-cloth at which the 'top brass' for this prestigious occasion in the Eardisley calendar were already gathered. Nearby, more tables were now decorated with the competition entries. I would be the judge later; I already had an idea of my final choices; one contest was for the best spring flower arrangement, the other for the most creative knitted 'scarecrow'! On one side and just in front of the curtained stage, a diminutive little lady was poised on the piano stool. I remember thinking that she had been there for quite a long while. She was waiting for her 'moment' when the President would ask her to play 'Jerusalem', the hymn which is traditionally sung at the beginning of every WI meeting. Opposite, were my birds. From time to time I saw individuals excitedly turning to one another as they suddenly realised their presence; I would see others standing up and hands being pointed as they were clearly taken by surprise.

My birds, in place before an audience arrived, and certainly with no one approaching them from behind, would remain absolutely still. Very occasionally the buzzard might shuffle her wings but, strangely, would always face away from those looking at her; the kestrel might bob his head once or twice, as he refocused on something new that took his interest; the tawny owl would, for no apparent reason, suddenly rotate his head through ninety degrees or more, and the pocket-sized female little owl would sit tight, her head and neck sunk deep into her shoulders. With a fixed and unnerving stare, she would scowl with such determination that she would, inevitably, become the talking point of the front rows.

Madam President had unobtrusively slipped over to confirm her planned order of proceedings as I waited patiently, watching the hustle and bustle. At that moment I was aware, out of the corner of my eye, of the tawny owl completing another, but quite slow, neck rotation. Few noticed except one particular lady, quite close by. Very conspicuous from her distinctive and eye-catching red jacket and black blouse, she turned and, clutching her neighbour by the sleeve, said, "'ere, I thought that owl was stuffed!"

"Don't be silly," her companion started, "of course they're not; they're alive; I've seen the big one move as well."

"You mean that eagle looking thing?" the lady in red interrupted.

"Yes, whatever it is, but I've seen it shuffling its feathers too." With that both women continued talking to their friends.

Yet again, I remembered Gerry's advice, which was never to let a fortuitous moment pass by, and to always involve the audience if possible to play their part. I promptly spoke to the members of the Institute sitting a couple of rows in front.

"Excuse me," I began, "I am sure I recognise the lady in red sitting behind you." I pointed discreetly.

Murphy's Law, the first two ladies had no idea, but within a matter of moments, I was told by others that, in fact, the lady in question was a Mrs Evans of Norton Canon Womens Institute. I thanked them and made a note of her name on the evening's flash card, along with the farm and woodland details I had noted earlier.

Official business over, the meeting was soon under way and I was formally introduced. All went well with the buzzard and kestrel and it wasn't long before I was in to my opening sequence with the tawny owl, "it's round about now that tawny owls will be stirring from their daytime slumber ..." Later in the sequence I discussed the owl's 'swivel' neck. My owl was so tame, that I reckoned he actually knew what I was going to say and when. He seemed fully aware of the way I explained a certain sequence to an audience. Of course, he had completed the procedure many times before.

Wearing a soft glove on my left hand, he would move his head to the left or right every time I flicked my thumb beneath the soles of his feet. Simultaneously, I would move my right hand sideways, horizontally, to the left or to the right, but always complementing the movement of his head. This evening was no different and in no time I was asking the front row, now occupied by all the Presidents, how many of them could see the line of cotton stretching from my right hand to the bird's neck, for that was how he rotated his neck whenever I moved my right hand! Of course no one had the faintest idea

of the role of my thumb; several Presidents leaned forward, whilst simultaneously pulling their glasses down onto the bridge of their nose, in an attempt to see the line of cotton. They hastily realised that I was only joking, but took my leg-pull in good grace. It was then that I thought it the right moment to make my move.

"Well, at least you realise," I said staring directly and only at the front rows, "that the owl is alive," and without raising my eyes I added, "unlike Mrs Evans of Norton Canon who thinks the bird is stuffed!"

With that the balloon went up. I saw a red-faced and distinctly mortified Mrs Evans being stared at by rows of ladies. I hurried on, unsure of the eventual outcome.

An hour later I had concluded. I then received a vote of thanks from another designated lady; my presentation had been well received. Yet another lady then took charge of me, for it was time to judge the competition entries. It was at that moment that I spotted the still flushed Mrs Evans making her way directly towards me through the jostling members.

'David,' I thought, 'just offer your profuse apologies.'

"I am so sorry," I began as she approached, "I never meant to embarrass you ..."

"No, no, not at all, Mr Chaffe," the lady interrupted. "You see, your remarks, well they were just fine. However my problem is, well," and she hesitated before continuing, "you see, I won't be able to hold my head high in County Hall again!"

I cannot explain why my owls have caused such havoc over the years in Herefordshire. I reminisce now about another Women's Institute meeting, another evening occasion, this time in the village of Moreton-on-Lugg. Well, it's not so much what happened during the meeting rather than the mishap that occurred outside the church hall in the main street.

I had hand-reared a female European eagle owl, a youngster from a clutch hatched in my collection. The parents were direct descendants of wild stock, imported by Philip Wayre from the coniferous forests of northern Finland in the early 1960s. 'Gonzo' greatly enhanced the owl group; with her penetrating orange-red eyes, her immense size and large wingspan, she brought a striking climax and conclusion to the hawk and owl presentation.

My Volkswagen one-ton van had been partitioned and 'double decked' to carry all the different combinations of bird and animal exhibits. The foxes and badgers were carried in adjacent purpose-built crates immediately above the engine, which was mounted in the rear of the vehicle; they were accessed through the rear tailgate. The birds, although never hooded, travelled on their lecture blocks.

The latter slotted rigidly into fixed timber ribbing, neither wobbling nor tilting, even when the breaking was severe. The birds were separated by hessian sacking panels in specially adapted spaces.

The eagle owl had one half of the floor of the vehicle, with the 'first team' of four travelling on the artificial floor above. She wasn't 'blocked', rather just tethered, travelling free on a deep bed of wood-shavings. There was a soft sacking 'door' which could either be drawn across tightly, or be loosened to reveal the whereabouts of the leash. With my gloved left hand securely holding that leash, and at the same time untying or tying it with my right hand, the bird had learnt either to spring clear from, or to jump back into, its special quarters.

Inevitably, and this summer's evening was no different, I had to leave my audience to fetch the bird. On my return, its sensational appearance and its powerful presence would immediately silence the assembled gathering.

There was no-one in sight as I approached my vehicle parked in the main street outside the hall. The eagle owl was instantly aware of her impending performance as she heard me opening the van door. Whenever I brought her free, she would flap her large wings three or four times, before shuffling and settling.

As she jumped clear this night, however, I noticed out of the corner of my eye a rather elderly gentleman cycling towards me on the opposite side of the street. There was no-one else around and, naturally, I glanced towards him to offer a passing acknowledge-

"... it was a glazed stare of incredulity as the eagle owl launched herself into her wing stretching routine!"

76

ment. Simultaneously, I remember seeing a look of utter amazement and shock on his face; it was a glazed stare of incredulity as the eagle owl launched herself into her wing-stretching routine.

The man continued cycling in the same direction, but he was progressively twisting his head back towards the owl as he went past and beyond me, and the fixed expression on his face never altered.

As I was entering the hall, I glanced at him again. By now his head was almost completely turned around. I backed through the entrance door, in order to shield the owl, and just at that moment, I heard a most almighty crash. I could see the spinning wheels of the upturned bicycle; the old boy had clearly suddenly lost

"...the old boy had been catapulted over the handlebars into the freshwater stream!"

www.cartoons4u.co.uk

control, had veered into the kerb and had been catapulted over the handlebars into the freshwater stream that ran alongside the length of the village street.

To my shame, I didn't stop or go to help but I hesitated just long enough to see a very wet, bedraggled and weed-covered person emerge from the water looking extremely confused. I felt unable to describe what had just happened to my waiting and expectant audience. Come to think of it he could have been the husband of one of the lady members! Nevertheless, I have related this event many times; and it has always been received with great hilarity.

I reckon the fellow was on his way, at his very regular time, to the village pub. The story of the 'one that got away' is probably the oldest in the book. Anglers continually, and especially so after several tipples, increase the length and weight of the fish caught on every occasion the tale is retold. I believe that many a similar yarn has since been recalled about this 'bloody great bird what I saw coming out of this van'. The eagle owl was probably identified as an eagle, and its wingspan, accompanied by the extended waving of arms as an extra and necessary illustration, has become bigger on every occasion. Of course, there has to be two other essential components to the story; firstly the number of pints consumed and secondly, the presence of eavesdropping and gullible strangers.

Of the man and the bent bicycle there was no sign at ten o'clock as I left for the Severn Bridge and eventually my home. However, I still reckoned it best to avoid stopping to enquire further!

The owl was the symbol of Pallas Athene, the patron of Athens and the goddess of wisdom. As we can see from ancient coins her owl was not just any owl, but the little owl. The scientific name it bears today, *Athene noctua,* confirms that the little owl is the goddess's 'wise old owl'.

In the early summer of 1968, the year after Peter Scott opened my Wildlife Park and British Nature Centre to the general public, three young little owls, just beginning to feather, were rescued close to Muchelney on the Somerset Levels, after an aged willow tree had unexpectedly collapsed.

The youngsters were lucky on two counts. Firstly, the tree had fallen into the field rather than toppling into the adjacent ditch, thus saving them from death by drowning. Secondly, the farmer regularly visited to check his fences because his store beef cattle were grazing these flower-rich summer meadows. The parent birds were nowhere to be seen; two small youngsters had not survived the crash, but three more advanced siblings, who were probably in the crown of the tree awaiting their parents' return, had been thrown clear. They were found perched on the broken branches of willow, well hidden by the dense foliage which had surely protected them from the prying eyes of carrion crows and foxes.

One of the three was very friendly and she was soon imprinted. A decision was quickly taken. Her sibling sister and brother, were to create an exhibit in one of the park's aviaries and she was to be specially tamed to 'meet' the public through my talks both in the Park and at my lectures.

I began to take her home. She became used to travelling; she would sit on a small rounded block in the kichen and quickly accepted the antics of my dogs, paid close attention to the television screen and observed and took in her stride all the various comings and goings.

At the time, I was living in Nempnett Thrubwell. My 'local' was the Live and Let Live public house in Blagdon, a village nestling beneath the Mendip Hills on the south side of Blagdon Lake.

One late autumn evening I called in on my way home and because of the conversation, I fetched the little owl into the public bar. The few locals were captivated. I just happened to place the bird on its block amongst the bottles of wine stacked on the bar counter. In this corner, sat Philip Cooper the pub's almost resident customer. His favourite tipple was rough Somerset cider which he drank relentlessly; he also chewed a pipe. I only ever saw him eat an occasional nugget of strong Cheddar cheese.

It wasn't long before the little owl was part of the bar fixtures whenever I was meeting friends for the evening, especially on a Friday or Saturday night. We would await patrons, particularly those coming from urban Bristol and Bath, and unused to the countryside and its ways. I recall now the occasion when two young couples arrived. One fellow came straight to the bar to order whilst his companions found a table. We were watching closely.

"Good evening, a dry martini with ice and lemon and a gin and tonic please; and what beers do you have on draught?"

"George's Boys Best from a Bristol brewery, and a local Mendip brew," landlord Bob Gulliver replied, as he prepared the two shorts.

"Two pints of George's then, please."

At that moment the fellow acknowledged Philip, the 'permanent' customer on his immediate left. At the same time he caught his first sight of and stared hard at the little owl on its block amongst the bottles. She scowled and glowered at him but didn't move one jot. The fellow took the first two drinks, came back, paid, took another long look at the owl, collected his change, and then with the two pints returned to the table.

female little owl; *Athene noctua,*.
"... she really could sit still and scowl and frown for a very long time ..."

"Do you see that owl on the bar?"

"What owl? Where?"

"There, next to the chap drinking the cider. D'ye see it, between the bottles of wine?"

"Don't be bloody stupid, that's not an owl. Well, it's not a *real* owl."

"I saw it blink, I really did."

"Pull the other one, it's got bells on."

Their conversation eventually turned to other matters, but I couldn't help noticing that from time to time all four kept checking the owl. I could make the tawny owl move its head; with the little owl it was entirely her decision if and when to move. She really could sit absolutely still for a very long time.

A little while later, there was an excited outburst from the next table. "The owl's head, it's facing the other way, so it must be alive," exclaimed one of the young women.

Now all four were staring very directly at the bird, and we, in turn were doing our utmost to appear unaware of their excitement and so avoided eye contact. We waited for the owl to make the next move. Suddenly, she turned her head very slowly back towards us and continued her direct stare.

"Well I'll be ******!" exclaimed one chap.

A little while later, the adjacent table were buying their next round of drinks.

"Same again?" said the second fellow to the others as he left the table. "Same again, please landlord," he announced approaching the bar. Now he paused and observed the owl. He looked very directly at her and then, turning to Philip, who was still chewing his pipe, said, "That owl. It is alive, isn't it?"

"You must be joking," said Philip, "I've never seen it move yet and I sit here every night!"

Chapter Five

"The seal actually took the fish from my fingers!"

Cow Atlantic Grey Seal; *Halichoerus grypus*
© John Threlfall 2007
www.johnthrelfall.co.uk

The old grey music doctors of the ocean,
their holy happy eyes shining devotion,
applaud and blow
in foam and soft commotion

source: *Grey Seal, Common Seal*
R.M. Lockley

Despite the extreme refinement of their physiology in respect to diving, the true seals (Common and Grey) are still not fully emancipated from theier terrestrial ancestors of some 25 million years ago. The tie to land or ice for birth and nurture of the youngsters sets the pattern of their lives.

source: The New Encyclopedia of Mammals, edited by David MacDonald, Oxford University Press.

Today, throughout the world ... eleven of the fifteen major fishing zones are in decline ... thirty per cent of fish species are also endangered.

source: Earth from the Air; a photographic portrait of our planet. Yann Arhus-Bertrand, 2006

Common Seals a male & female
have hauled themselves out on the
Shingle

Blakeney Point is home to a thriving
population of Grey & Common Seal

Two Sandwich Tern & a
Ringed Plover are by
these two Common Seal
& give some idea of Siz

Grey Seal have
a Strong Roman
nose & are bigger
than Common Seal

The Bull Grey is still
Wet & looks much
Blacker than the
females.

GREY SEAL a young pup is in
company with a bull & 2 cows

Common Seal have a more Dog like
kindley face than the Grey Seals.

© Steve Cale, 2007. www.steve-cale-artist.co.uk

The telegram was brief and to the point.

Arrangements had to be hastily made; I needed to decide immediately where best to keep this youngster on my return and, at that moment, I had no idea whether it was still suckling or had been weaned onto solid food. My only previous experience in hand rearing seal pups had been whilst working with Philip Wayre in Norfolk some years previously. Then, after mid-summer gales had struck the sandbanks of the Wash and the shingle ridges around Blakeney Point, some dozen individuals had been brought in. Although we tried very hard, losses were high. Sadly, nearly all the pups had been injured during the bad weather; nevertheless, one animal was successfully reared after much painstaking care.

One necessity had clearly stuck in my mind from that first experience. It was essential that any holding pen or crèche was kept as clean as possible. Ideally, that meant having a concreted area with enough space for two or more adjacent enclosures. A pup would need to be regularly shepherded into a new space and the soiled floor, with its urine and faeces, hosed clean; all this had to be completed without unduly frightening the pup. In Norfolk, unfortunately, we received too many pups at one time so space was limited. I planned to create a 'nursery', with straw bales acting as flexible walls, to achieve the vital speed of movement which would contribute to a successful outcome.

Straw bales answered another important requirement. I wanted to spend much time with this newcomer. By sitting on or leaning back against a bale, I would be almost level with the pup; it wouldn't be frightened by the overpowering shape caused by stand-

Sweet wind, so bitter-sweet for me,
Go gently now for you are free
To dance those longing years away,
And blend your song with scent and spray,
With low sea-tunes abrim with words
Of Skokholm's lonely isle of birds.

On Visiting Skokholm, Frances Stephenson

The island of Skokholm, secured for the future ... gwarchod e'r dyfodol ... on the 7th April 2006, was also home to Ronald Lockley and his family during the 1930s.

Photograph © Sid Howells

ing over it. It was important for my shape to resemble as much as possible its mother with which the pup had its first visual contact. This pup would be destined for display at my Wildlife Park; I wanted my young visitors to hand-feed it, under supervision, so quickly earning its total confidence was paramount. Twenty-five years later, Storm, my otter cub, grew into the remarkable creature she eventually became because I spent countless hours playing with her in an untidy bed of loose straw, thus winning her complete confidence.

Our double garage was requisitioned. The sliding doors would allow in light and fresh air; the temporary outer wall would now be two straw bales high, well tied together. Inside access was from the back staircase which led to my father's drawing offices directly above. There was mains power, and electric light to assist night-time feeding and for just spending time with the pup. Finally, and most importantly, there was an internal water standpipe.

So, in theory, it was all systems go! My close friend, Mike Lubbock, a talented aviculturist at the Wildfowl Trust was to stay overnight before accompanying me to West Wales. I recall he always seemed able to take time off at a moment's notice! However, I had an unresolved problem. In an accident I had smashed the nearside headlight of my Commer one-ton van; the replacement and repairs

Naturalist, Ronald Lockley, the first to pioneer studies of manx shearwaters and storm petrels, on his island home of Skokholm in the 1930s

had been booked but because of the urgent need to respond to Lockley's telegram, I gambled on placing a large torch on a concrete block in the footwell. The torch was aligned so that the beam would shine through the gap. Surely the chances were against the restricted light being spotted by the police. But, our luck ran out, and not for the first time when moving seals.

I had first come across the name of Ronald Lockley by reading his books. In *The Island* he describes his life on Skokholm during the 1930s, of being alone with his wife Doris and young daughter, with only occasional seasonal helpers and the resident lighthouse keepers for company. Fortunately, for him, the family were blessed by the misfortune of the *Alice Williams*, a schooner, which foundered on the island. Her cargo surrendered a bonus of some seventy tons of coal giving them ample supplies of fuel along with quantities of timbers washed onto the rocks from the boat's decks and hull; Lockley was able to restore the derelict farmhouse and outbuildings.

It was on Skokholm, along with the neighbouring islands of Skomer and Grassholm, the latter with its vast colony of gannets, that Lockley pursued his studies of nesting guillemots, razorbills, puffins and kittiwakes. They were his spring and summer neighbours; there were also large colonies of the secretive manx shearwaters and storm petrels. The desire to unravel the latter's complex winter orientations across the world's oceans excited the man who became one of the 20th century's most respected and accomplished naturalists.

Native also to that part of the Welsh coast are large numbers of breeding Atlantic grey seals; calving in September and October the thirty pound pups, covered in a white hair coat at birth, are born on remote beaches in inaccessible and unexplored caves. The pups are dropped on the shingle and sand well above normal high tide levels. So rich and dense is the cow seal's milk, that within three weeks the

'Claudia', a female (cow) Atlantic Grey seal, *Halichoerus grypus*, originally storm-washed off Pembrokeshire and hand reared by the author, during the autumn of 1968.

pups will be weaned at ninety pounds. Three weeks later and a much slimmer sixty pound pup, having moulted into a blotched grey fur coat, the male or bull pup is already distinctly darker, is ready to first experience the open sea and to learn to fend for itself. This rapid increase in weight would prove the biggest hurdle to overcome when I attempted to hand-rear storm-washed orphans. As each wild pup makes its way into the environment of the open sea and combats the dangers of ever-strengthening winter gales, its mother, whose milk will by now have dried up, will be mating with the harem's master bull for the following autumn's calving.

In the 1950s, Lockley moved to the Orielton Estate on mainland west Pembrokeshire. I met him there for the first time. I can still clearly remember the drive past the lake where, and I was not to know then, wild otters lived. We talked at length. I felt close to a naturalist about whose way of life I had only previously imagined through his writings. Here was a quiet and very well-informed person, making special time for a youngster who, other than from a request by letter, was a complete stranger. I left captivated and inspired.

I had been similarly befriended by Peter Scott at Slimbridge; Scott and Lockley were lifelong friends. A decade later, Lockley knew of my plans to create my Wildlife Park when I came down from Cambridge.

Peter Scott had kindly agreed to open the Wildlife Park; both were present that June summer evening in 1967. Now, this seal pup in July 1966, whose origins I would shortly discover, was Lockley's first but not his last contribution to the Park's future success and to my plans and lifetime's work.

"Dick's a strapping young male common seal pup; he should do well," Lockley announced as the three of us took in the view. Lockley never failed to enjoy this landscape; his beloved Skokholm with the Island of Skomer lying nearer, were both somewhat lost in a summer haze over the blue Atlantic swell on that early August afternoon. Mike and I were then introduced to Dick who certainly appeared very lively and in good health; we learned that he had been rescued some six weeks previously after storms on the East coast, sparking memories for me of my Norfolk experiences five years previously.

Lockley explained how female common seals can hold their pregnancy; that some eighty percent of pups are born on the evening tide of midsummer's night; that they are dropped at the top of the tide, in the hour of slack water that divides the flow and ebb. The mothers disperse to wash and clear any after-birth; then return to be reunited with their offspring. If the pups were to be born on a still strong-flowing incoming or ebbing tide, they could be scattered by the longshore drift. Mother seals could spend hours searching with many pups eventually becoming abandoned.

"... gannets drifting lazily between the troughs of the waves ... occasionally they would climb steeply and hang on the wind before plunging in with folded wings to fish ..."

Inevitably, it was later than we planned before we finally loaded Dick into the van. He was soon lost amongst the loose straw. During the long uneventful journey bringing home one of the first 'star' exhibits for my Wildlife Park, I recalled that other highly significant episode in mid-Wales when I returned with my first bantams from the Tregaron Bog.

Dick had soon dried out; the grey blotches on his silvery grey coat had faded, paling into a dense fur that was now tinged with cream.

The only remaining wet patches of fur were around his eyes as his tear ducts worked overtime. Occasionally, he gazed at us through soulful and trusting eyes, but for most of the journey he had rolled over onto one side and was asleep, apparently unconcerned by the movement of the vehicle. Lockley had told us to continue to force-feed him with a tube directly into his stomach, funnelling in the milk enriched with cod liver oil, begun when Dick was first found and which he had continued. His body weight had increased significantly, although perhaps not at the rate if he had been suckling his wild mother. Nevertheless, Dick's emerging pristine fur coat was testimony to a successful process. Lockley had advised us, too, that the time was also fast approaching for his

Adult common or harbour seal, *Phoca vitulina*, hauled out at Blakeney Point, on the north Norfolk coast.

© John and Tracy Langley, Chester
www.ourwildlifephotography.co.uk

pup to be weaned onto solid food; he suggested sourcing fish merchants for sprats and small herring and mackerel. Clearly, whilst successfully settling Dick into the confines of the garage, continuing his feeds and, most importantly, spending time with him, finding fish suppliers would be another priority the following day.

"Stand by for some fun," was Mike's opening remark at gone eleven o'clock and with the journey's end in sight.

Approaching rapidly from behind on the A38 was the blue flashing light of a police patrol car; in no time, I was winding down the driver's window to answer the questions I knew were coming.

I had planned my strategy; I would apologise, telling the officers that repairs to the headlamp were in hand. This was partially true. However, an emergency had arisen. A seal pup, washed up on the Welsh coast, had been offered to the Wildlife Park. I would not mention the seal had been found on the Wash and was now recovering. I also reckoned that the police would not know the difference between common and Atlantic grey seals.

I was proven right; the officers accepted my apologies for the virtual light failure, even smiling at our attempts to plug the gap with a torch. They were fascinated by Dick, who played his part by showing great curiosity in these intruders in dark blue.

'You'd best get this little chap to bed.' With that the police wished Dick, us and the Wildlife Park well for the future.

We finally put the lights out on my first seal pup at 1.00am. Mum and Dad had waited up for our return. There was relief for a successful journey. Next morning both Doug Brokenbrow, a fish

Diane, a Common seal, *Phoca vitulina*, rescued from the Wash after summer storms, and hand-reared in the summer of 1966.
© Jim Hale; courtesy of Mia Hale

merchant of long-standing in the city's Fish Market, and Robin Crick, working for a competitor, but a friend and contemporary from Clifton days, found a few frozen sprats as a stop-gap supply. I also made my first approaches to the Brixham and Torbay Fish Company; I needed to buy in bulk quayside. Eventually, I would travel to Newlyn and Milford Haven. In Grimsby, Petersen was my merchant; I would buy a hundred stone of small herring landed in Stornoway the previous day from trawlers working the Minch in the Outer Hebrides.

However, the main challenge was to introduce Dick to his first solid food. Again, I followed Lockley's instructions closely. I rolled Dick in a blanket, tightly, so that only the very front of his head was poking out of one end. Ideally, the blanket needed to finish just behind his eyes and ears. At the same time, I had to be in a position so that my knees were either side of his neck. The secret then was to gently insert from one side a short length of broom handle into the back of the mouth. This was covered in cricket bat handle rubber to prevent damage to the young teeth and causing the tender gums to bleed. Controlling Dick with my knees and holding the handle with my left hand set up the best position from which to try and slip a sprat down the back of his throat.

We found feeding him with the tube straightforward. It was a different ball game when we tried a few thawed sprats. We were becoming very frustrated when suddenly the timing worked and the first fish slipped down Dick's open throat. Half a dozen more quickly followed with halibut oil capsules added to a couple, another of Lockley's ideas to boost Dick's vitamin intake. We were on our way!

Mike left for Slimbridge after lunch; he also had been thrilled to meet R M Lockley. Starting to feed Dick had been a difficult challenge successfully overcome. Mike was, and still is, a natural with wild crea-

Dick, an orphaned Common seal, *Phoca vitulina*, rescued from the same summer storm as Diane, was hand-reared by Ronald Lockley and the author in the summer of 1966.
© Jim Hale; courtesy of Mia Hale

tures, especially wildfowl. These days his aviculutural expertise and enthusiasm is widely recognised throughout the USA, their gain but sadly, our loss.

I kept Dick company very late into his second night; I had to pinch myself to believe that the scenario in front of me was for real. Inevitably, I recalled my first meeting with a seal, which prompted my first letter to Ronald Lockley. But that was no creature like Dick; it was an Atlantic grey which I came upon in a magical and wild environment. I still go to the very same place over fifty years later!

Family holidays during the early 1950s, always taken in the first fortnight in September, were spent at the Grenville Hotel in Bude, north Cornwall. My uncle and aunt, John and Elsie Rowe, Elsie was my mother's elder sister, along with my cousin Patrick made up the family party. Pat and I would spend the mornings trying to improve our surfing skills at Crooklets Beach; in the afternoons we discovered the various small marine life, shore crabs and the occasional bullhead, from amongst the rock pools and an enclosed tidal swimming pool that was part of the breakwater protecting the beach. We also learned to row along the canal; the lock gates gave direct access to the open sea at high water. Here was the evidence of the once flourishing port and quayside which saw coal, timber and limestone imported from the south Wales ports.

From Bude I first saw magical Lundy; some days it appeared so close; at other times it was suddenly lost from view as low cloud and misty rain drifted in from the western Atlantic. Before our second annual holiday I had already landed on the island, after travelling on one of the Campbells paddle-steamers which carried day-trippers to the Bristol Channel harbours from Bristol's Hotwells dock.

I knew the three islands of Skomer, Skokholm and Grassholm lay to the north-west over the horizon because of the birds I saw. There were often long lines of gannets drifting lazily between the troughs of the waves, always heading south-west; occasionally they would climb steeply and hang on the wind before plunging in with folded wings on a potential target. Whilst being amazed by these master fishers I would suddenly spot the manx shearwaters and storm petrels, invisible without field glasses. How many more did I miss during the days of strong winds when the spume blew off the top of the turbulent waves? If I wasn't gazing at gannets, then there were other birds much closer to hand. I could easily separate shags from cormorants now; lost amongst the seaweed covered rocks I would suddenly have amazing close-ups of oyster catcher and dunlin. On Widemouth Beach, our golden retriever, Whisper, was always chasing the wavelets as they retreated from amongst the rocks. She would flush sedate ringed plover and the wave-chasing sanderling.

These were so close I couldn't fail to identify them. Meanwhile, the solid and chunky little waders with the short orange legs, turnstones, would always ignore Whisper's close scrutiny.

"Look, a curlew," I said on one occasion; it didn't immediately fly; it was clearly thinking if the turnstones aren't going to fly...

"Can't be a curlew," my father interrupted, "it's got a straight bill; in fact, it turns up slightly at the end; and I've seen enough curlews to know it's a different colour. Look at its slightly reddish plumage."

My *Observers Book of Birds* had been hugely reinforced by the *Handbook of British Birds*, compiled by Witherby, Jourdain, Ticehurst and Tucker and edited by PAD Hollom. Back at the hotel and with such close-up images fresh in my mind, I would surely achieve a definite identification.

"It was a black-tailed godwit," I announced confidently; "the reddish plumage is the last of its summer breeding plumage; there's another very similar bird but with a clearly upcurved bill, the bar-tailed godwit. But we were so close there can be no mistake."

We had suffered continual wet weather one year so decided to try somewhere new. I'll never forget my first sight of the French and Belgian crabbers lying off Smeaton's Pier, in St Ives Bay; the 'local' inshore mackerel boats were at anchor in long rows across the inner harbour. We explored the narrow streets, walked to the chapel on the island, and had our packed lunch sitting on the crab and lobster pots stacked on the quay. It was a wrench to leave and very late by the time we had returned to our hotel. We never did holiday in Bude again; twenty-five years later my family owned 1 Quay Street, one of only three cottages whose basements, originally sail lofts, led directly onto the harbour beach. Here, Olivia would swim most days on her return from school.

On yet another wet day the next summer, Dad and I followed a track past the coastguard cottages towards Gurnards Head; a rugged footpath led to a secluded cove. We skirted abandoned granite structures last used when the area was mined for its deposits of tin. Amongst the great slabs of granite, later covered by the high tides, we discovered a flooded vent shaft. The sea was a cobalt blue, with a swell punctured only by the sound of breakers

Grey seal pups are born, weighing around 30lbs, in caves in Cornwall around September time and on inaccessible pebbly beaches in West Wales a month or so later. On the Farne Islands and in north Norfolk, they are calved much later in the year, around November and December.
© Nick Martin www.martinimages.co.uk

90

"... a very large and roman nosed pale head appeared from nowhere. The seal had probably been bottling ..."

'skimming' the pebbles on a beach out of sight below. Only an occasional gull mewed plaintively as we waited in an eery silence.

I still have no idea for how long two large soulful eyes had been staring at us. A very large and roman-nosed head of a grey seal was just feet away, having appeared from nowhere. I now know it had been 'bottling', sleeping vertically over a period of about twenty minutes and was below the surface when we arrived. When seals run short of oxygen they have an ability, through a simple valve system, to switch to stored-up carbohydrates. Pale grey with dark blotches she was an adult cow, and likely to soon give birth to her single pup in some nearby remote cave; with an access facing the open ocean the entrance, below water at both high and low tide, would lead to a dark and sheltered pebbly beach. There she would suckle her pup for up to three weeks.

Our companion teased and captivated us. Without warning, she then slipped away. I was thinking, 'what a remarkable hour,' when suddenly from nowhere there were some gannets close by; within moments there was a raucous din, as they plunged repeatedly into a shoal of fish. In no time, they had moved on as the prey species dispersed deeper to avoid their persistent and deadly attacks.

Many years later, I would know that this bay is a haven and a source of food for both seals and certain seabirds. At the turn of every year grey mullet swarm in large shoals. The west Cornwall seals congregate here; after a month of easy feeding, they complete their annual moult. One of my fish merchants, Whitfields' of Milford Haven, could always supply herring in the fortnight before Christmas. Herring seasonly

Brutus, a 'bull' Atlantic grey seal, one of the two pups rescued from Pembrokeshire and hand-reared by the author in the autumn of 1968, here heading to his regular afternoon feed in the Wildlife Park.

mass like grey mullet; the seals of the west Wales coast have an easy and rich supply of food, too. In north Pembrokeshire, close to Newport, where the Nevern estuary meets the sea, there is a pebbly beach below steep cliffs where over two hundred animals will gather for their annual moult; this is the largest haul-out of grey seals south of the Farne Islands. Pwll Coch, or the 'Red Wilderness', was discovered by Ronald Lockley in the early years of World War Two.

In the late summer of '66, Dick was joined by another hand-reared common seal pup. Lockley's grapevine was clearly working. She had been orphaned in the same mid-summer gales but had stayed in Lincolnshire. We called her Diane and she was already feeding well; we immediately created a double creche and provided a tin bath in which both pups became used to water; it was fixed at an angle and the water was changed constantly; both loved to put their faces against the hose enjoying the stimulus of the fresh water.

Life became hectic in the garage. By mid October, we were struggling to stomach-feed two Atlantic grey pups which had been rescued in quick succession off the Pembrokeshire coast. I had collected both within days of each other from Maendewi Farm at Whitesands Bay. Here my friends, Terry and Anne Davies, kept sheep and store beef cattle; Terry was a crew member on the nearby St Justinian lifeboat at St Davids and in his own boat, which was on permanent station at Marloes, he ran the stores and summer visitors to the islands of Skokholm and Skomer.

The first pup had been picked up by a fishing boat homeward bound to Milford as she slid through the tidal race between Ramsey Island and the mainland. The second had been spotted by a walker with her dog on Newgale beach. Both were lucky pups; both were rescued soon after being washed from their natal beach or cave; both had avoided serious injury from being tossed and crushed against the rocks and both were in the right place at the right time.

The two 'greys' were a real handful; they were much larger and stronger than Dick and Diane; although of a good body weight we still had to come close to the incredible growth they would achieve when suckling their wild mother. The late Robin Jones, my trusted senior member of staff and I, would have a battle royal twice every working day. It was like controlling two fifty pound bags of aggressive ferrets! We were regularly bitten, our clothing would be badly ripped and, inevitably, we were soaked in the rich oily feed. Sweat would pour off us! I fondly remember both occasions when the pups first took whole fish. Halibut oil, yeast and calcium tablets were regularly added, and the pups progressed steadily. Lockley often called; he was then living in Colyton, in South Devon. He would sit for some time gazing at the pups, staggered at the effort and time we were spending with all four, especially the two greys. He was often quiet; his mind was elsewhere; he was on an island somewhere!

So, now, there were four youngsters to befriend at night. I had to proceed quickly with the construction and landscaping of two seal pools. Robin had conceived the brilliant idea of constructing a dam on the River Trym which, when constructed, would allow us to pump ample quantities of water to the pools. In fact, it was on this deep water where my whooper swans would successfully rear their cygnets. Both pools had exit pipes controlled by expandable screw bungs, allowing them to be emptied quickly.

It was clear that Dick and Diane were the two seals to be fed by hand. It was essential that their pool was built so that youngsters could hand-feed them. Robin constructed a semi-circular retaining wall to the pool, capped it with paving and assembled a restraining fence with an overhang. By standing on the top of the wall the youngsters could stretch forward over the fence as the seals slid ashore onto a natural pebbly beach; the wall and beach were flush with the water. Seal feeding time became the star attraction; unlike the sea lion feeds at Bristol Zoo, where rows of people were crushed close to a keeper dressed in regulation grey uniform with peaked cap, I planned something different. My staff would help each youngster give a seal a fish, whilst I presented a resumé on the life cycle of seals and the personal life of each character in the pool. I had no plans for the grey seals to be hand-fed; they were far too boisterous. Nevertheless, they would haul themselves to the high ground behind their boundary fence to be fed; again my talks with those watching would be factual, yet anecdotal, and would inevitably mention Lockley's significant role.

At 3.30pm every afternoon, especially during school holidays and at weekends, youngsters would gather excitedly. I would brief them from my vantage point, a large almost square rock on the opposite side of the pool and from which, before commencing, I always had to move Dick. Firstly, the youngsters would turn together to be given their fish; then they would turn back together, importantly keeping their fish out of sight, to face the pool. The seals were patrolling, waiting expectantly. Each youngster would, in turn, lean out holding a fish in one hand whilst keeping the other hand on the rail. Finally, they would drop the fish into the mouth of one of the waiting seals. Anyway, that was plan A; most times, however it was Plan A gone wrong!

As the seals ranged back and forth, the water flowed over the youngsters' feet; some panicked and threw their fish into the water, but most stood their ground and fed their favourite individual.

My mother would report on the success of the seal feeding. On Sunday afternoons, always our busiest day, she would lend a hand in the cafe, serving teas and ice creams. We would recruit students from the VIth form of the nearby secondary school in Henbury. The girls coped well, but in the half hour after 'seal feeding' they could be rushed off their feet. My mother provided the calm head. She would also listen to visitors' comments. Mothers and grandparents would have previously selected their table either inside or outside the cafe to await their children's return. Fathers had joined the youngsters

Plan 'A' gone wrong! Feeding a seal created lifetime memories for youngsters ... and for some fathers, too!

at the seal pool; inevitably, it was they who were left behind to ask more questions as their youngsters fled in an excited stampede.

"It was great;" "the seal actually took the fish from my fingers;" "the water came right over my shoes and I'm sopping wet;" "I've got to come again," which was frequently followed by, "well alright, but we'll have to ask your father." Nearly all of the comments were similar to this.

"I was frightened;" "ugh, my hand smells of fish;" "I've got wet socks and feet," accompanied by, "well, I haven't got any spare ones so you'll just have to put up with it!" would summarise the rest.

Feeding Dick and Diane at close quarters was, without doubt, although I did not realise it at the time, the first step in creating the Wildlife 'Face to Face' experience; personal participation in feeding a seal created lifetime memories for youngsters, and for some fathers, too!

I know the secret to that achievement. That autumn when the pups were in the garage, my father would accompany builders and clients down the back staircase after a meeting and took great pride in continuing his conversation with, "you really won't believe what David's caring for in the garage. Have a guess." Imagine their utter surprise as they were confronted by not one but four pairs of appealing eyes staring over the straw bales. Imagine too, my mother's typical opening remark at supper sometimes, "I suppose you took everybody in to see the seals, did you?" Nevertheless, the seals enjoyed the evening company and receiving fish from the more brave or, should I say, more foolhardy strangers. Unwittingly, the seals were beginning to associate people with food; the seeds to thousands of memorable seal feeds in the Wildlife Park had been sown.

Early on a summer's day in 1968 one of my staff, carrying out the morning's rounds, discovered an awful tragedy.

It was vital that the water in the seal pools was always as clean as possible. We used a heavy but portable, electric

Grey seals frequently haul out on sandbars and pebbly beaches; researchers can exploit such occasions to identify distinctive head patterns
© Nick Martin www.martinimages.co.uk

monopump to bring in the clean water held behind the river dam. We would place the pump on the retaining wall of the pen, where the youngsters would stand; We could empty in twenty minutes and refill in two hours; one pipe was in the deep river water, the other stretched into the bottom of the pool. Both seals would enjoy the sensation of the incoming water as it swirled around them; they clearly recalled the tin bath in the garage.

Overnight some individuals had broken into the Park; Dick and Diane always slept hauled out on the pebble beach; they were oblivious to people; the pump was raised and thudded into Diane ...

I am still unable to find the words to describe the scene that morning; forty years later I still cannot understand the minds and actions of those people. Roger Mills, the interviewer for the BBC's evening regional news programme, was reduced to tears as the cameras recorded the dreadful images.

Over recent years grey seals have moved south in increasing numbers from the Farne Islands off Northumberland. Now, they also breed around the turn of the year on the sandbanks of Blakeney Point, in north Norfolk.

© Nick Martin www.martinimages.co.uk

I have not looked forward to recalling the loss of Diane since my conception of the *Face to Face with nature* story. I know the reader will understand if I pen no more, but will, at the same time, also appreciate my contempt for those involved then and towards others today who still harbour a similar attitude towards and disdain for the life of a wild creature.

The loss of Diane made national news headlines. Within days, I had been telephoned by George Cansdale, director of Skegness Marineland, offering three yearling female pups to give Dick a new family; they were orphans, all rescued from the Wash sandbanks.

George Cansdale, a well-known 'face' from presenting his television series about zoos, was a kind man and clearly doted on his seals. As Jonathan, my member of staff and I loaded the pups, I recalled fetching Dick from Pembrokeshire. These pups, too, were also in a bed of loose straw, enclosed by straw bales. Just before we pulled away, George opened the nearside side-loading door to take one final look at his three departing friends; however, as he bade farewell he failed to pull the door completely shut.

Our journey home began along Skegness seafront in the middle of summer; there were holiday-makers everywhere. At the first roundabout I heard a clunk.

"What was that?" I asked Jonathan.

"Nothing," he said a few moments later after peering into the nearside wing mirror, "I can't see anything."

Seconds later, there was a horn blaring as a car passed me. As I slowed, a fellow shouted from the open front passenger window.

"Something has just fallen out of your van back there. At the roundabout. It looked like a sealion!"

I stopped and told Jonathan to get out.

"The side door's open, and there are only two seals," he stumbled.

"Get back to the roundabout!" I shouted, "and stay with it. Now. Go on, move. I'll try and turn around."

However, there was no way I could avoid going to the following roundabout before coming back. When I next saw Jonathan he was doing something very similar to a Morris dance as he tried to keep the pup from straying onto the road; in fact, the beach and the North Sea weren't that far away! I came around the roundabout; I thought, 'blow the traffic' and stopped. I grabbed the seal by her hind flippers, you can only move seals 'in a hurry' that way, and holding her 'head downwards'. I shouted, "open the side door," as Jonathan hurried in front of me. In one movement, I swung the pup into the van. "I'll shut the door this time, you just get in."

The new arrivals learned very quickly from Dick and were soon playing their full part at feeding time. I never allowed the public to forget Diane's cruel death; neither did Dick forget. He never slept on their pebble beach again.

"I'll shut the door this time
- you just get in!"

Chapter Six

"We have a safety issue with customers using the 'chipper'."

Red Fox, *Vulpes vulpes*
© John Threlfall, 2007
www.johnthrelfall.co.uk

In Aesop's fable the cunning fox outwits the stork; the hero of the medieval tales of Reynard the Fox always gets the better of his adversary, the wolf; and in the children's fables of Beatrix Potter, the sly, sinister fox fools the gullible bird Jemima Puddle-Duck. The fact that foxes figure as the wily character in the popular tales of many cultures reflects their resourceful behaviour.

Foxes catch rodents with a characteristic 'mouse leap', springing off the ground and diving, front paws first, onto the prey. This aerial descent may be a device to counter the vertical jump used by some mice to escape predators. Red foxes catch earthworms that leave their burrows on warm, moist nights by criss-crossing pastures at a slow walk and listening for the rasping of the worm's bristles on the grass. Once a worm is detected, the fox poises over it before plunging its snout into the grass. Worms, whose tails retain a grip in their burrows, are not broken but gently pulled taut after a momentary pause, a highly effective technique that foxes have in common with fishermen collecting bait.

source: The New Encyclopedia of Mammals, edited by David Macdonald. Oxford University Press

Holkham Hall in North Norfolk has
for many years had a large heard of mainly spotted Fallow Deer.

These days the numbers of Pink
-footed Geese wintering have
increased greatly & sometimes they
will even feed in the park with the
fallow deer

Lapwing & Pink Feet
visit the park.

A fine Fallow Deer shows off
his super palmated Antlers.
During the Rut in late
Autumn the animals are at
their finest.

Steve Cale
2007

"Got him. This little beauty better be a buck."

At four o'clock in the afternoon, three of my staff, Robin Jones, Marcus Beaven and John Dawson and I had been on the Holkham Hall Estate close to the north Norfolk coast since early morning. The Vth Earl of Leicester had generously given me permission to collect a trio of Fallow deer fawns. Every year, inevitably, many had to be culled, so keeping the herd's numbers in check and avoiding the damage from over-grazing. Importantly, the Holkham herd was made up of pale spotted or true menil adults, with few of the darker dun or brownish-grey variety. It was the calves of the former which I planned to bottle-feed to create a striking exhibit in one of the woodland enclosures of my Wildlife Park.

We should have taken travelling crates, I had been told that, for moving deer, the crates needed an entrance and/or exit at both ends as it was important not to have to reach in to try and turn a creature. They needed to be long and very narrow so as to avoid a limb or neck being trapped with fatal consequences. With no such crate available, I decided to tie both front and back legs together and place the fawns in hessian sacks filled with loose straw. Only their heads would be exposed and I would darken the van's windows to keep them calm during the long journey home.

We made an inauspicious start. Armed with several lengths of fruit netting and some light stakes, we had approached an area of

An adult Fallow deer hind, *Dama dama*; nearly all of the Holkham Hall herd were of the pale spotted or true menil type.
© David Chapman, 2007. www.davidchapman.org.uk

99

We kept the two Holkham fallow hind fawns especially close, so they would always be hand tame.
© Jim Hale 1966, courtesy Mia Hale

dense undergrowth where, by mid-July, there were extensive tall and dense nettlebeds. We identified the runs made by the adult hinds; we staked three, we only had three nets, and moved gently forward whilst continually flicking the vegetation. Suddenly, a hind would explode out of cover with a bouncing, almost staccato gait. Some disappeared, a few would travel about thirty yards before stopping, turning and facing us; but there was no sign of any fawns. When we repeated the procedure exactly the same thing happened.

We took stock and drew up plan B. We guessed, correctly, that if a hind bolted and turned, then she had a fawn which was staying absolutely still. There was no alternative but to go directly into the nettlebeds. We had to be successful on at least three occasions. I wanted to return with a buck and two hind fawns, so we had to brave the discomfort from the stings. Our technique had to come right that morning; we could not afford to keep any fawns tied for more than twenty-four hours. They would need to be released into one of the Park's stables by the following evening.

I had two factors on my side; Robin Jones and lady luck. Robin was very durable. It was his suggestion to abandon the nets and to push through the waist-high nettles. It was critical for our success that Robin saw the crouching fawn first because he would never hesitate; he would have it smothered with front and back legs held before Marcus and I had even reacted. Robin had an innate instinct first learnt as a youngster on the family farm near Westbury-sub-Mendip, and later from a couple of years spent as a ranger in the game parks of Kenneth Kaunda's Zambia.

Soon our, I mean Robin's, first capture was safely aboard the vehicle. Now for two more. I can't recollect how many different swathes of nettles through which we stealthily crept with no success. We spotted two more fawns, the second was another hind calf. Exhausted, we hadn't stopped for a break all day, we finally hit the jackpot. The male fawn was only the third we had discovered, after a dismal start we had, amazingly, bagged all three youngsters which we had flushed.

We overnighted with Bob and Joan Cooke; we checked the fawns regularly and after a long uneventful journey home we gently untied them. Although experiencing cramp initially, they were soon standing steadily. An infra-red light was left on all night and we began to bottle feed with Ostermilk No 2 early the next morning. All three became hand tame and were fine specimens of the pale variety. They would readily come to the pen's fence to be fed cattle nuts by visitors; they bred well and the herd was a much admired sight.

It had been a fortunate day; sadly, Robin was not so lucky in life. Helen and I met him, some years later, just before his untimely death; he was a mere shadow of the hardy 'fun' man who played so important a role in the creation and the success of the Wildlife Park. I shall always be grateful to him and I treasure his memory.

I was suffering an anxious wait in the cargo handling bay at Bristol's Lulsgate Airport for an arrival from Glasgow Airport. I had long completed the endless paperwork and had been told that a large travelling crate would soon be at the exit. I was keen to see the occupant, a red deer stag calf, which was still being bottle-fed.

I had taken a gamble on accepting him. I already knew that the male calves of all the larger deer found in the UK, red, sika, fallow and roe, and called stags or bucks, can be treacherous 'in the rut' if they have been hand-reared. Accordingly, my first red deer calves were an unrelated trio that I fetched from the annual round-up of parent-reared youngsters out of the Warnham Court herd in Sussex. On my return, I had opened the back doors of the van and all three 'bounced' into their woodland enclosure. After some fifty yards both hind calves stopped; the stag calf, however, continued and when confronted by the outer fence of the enclosure, which was also the Park's boundary fence, took one brief look and, without hesitation, cleared the six foot barrier, overhang and all!

Several 'experts' suggested that he would just hang around the perimeter fence, waiting to rejoin his companions. Even at four months of age he was a strapping and handsome beast but, strangely, there were no sightings and we never saw him again. Eventually, however, he did reappear. Just before

Sannox, the orphaned Red deer, *Cervus elaphus*, stag calf from the Isle of Arran, was still being bottle-fed when he arrived at the Wildlife Park.

Christmas, Geoff Doran, my vet, was on a routine visit to Berkeley Castle and its hunt kennels and stables. He was informed that a 'stranger' had at first attached itself to the Castle's herd, before eventually becoming fully integrated. There was little doubt he was the calf we had only momentarily admired!

In stark contrast, the two Warnham hinds settled completely into their new life; I hoped that during the following summer I would be fortunate to hear of an orphaned calf; if it was another hind calf, so be it, but a stag calf would be a great bonus. I trawled the national press; friends and contacts kept eyes and ears to the ground, all to no avail. Then, from a source still unknown, came a telephone call from the estate office of the Scottish Forestry Commission on the island of Arran. Ten minutes later, having put caution and previous good advice aside, I had accepted the offer of Sannox. He had been found on the high ground lying alongside his mother who had sadly met a tragic end. Although still being bottle-fed, he was now rapidly becoming independent; he needed a new home and there was no way that he was going to be allowed back 'on the hill'; now an outcast, he would not survive his first winter.

One of our Warnham Court Red deer hinds with her hind calf. Both adults bred every summer, their progeny sired by Sannox.
© Nick Martin, 2007. www.martinimages.co.uk

Sannox's journey began on Arran by Land Rover to Brodick Quay; then it was the Caledonian MacBrayne ferry to the mainland harbour of Adrossan, before road transport again to Glasgow Airport and the final flight. The Forestry Commission met all the costs.

We continued to bottle feed Sannox but soon weaned him onto a coarse dairy ration which we fed to our six species of native deer; along with fresh root vegetables, it proved to be a successful substitute diet and eventually, five species of deer regularly bred; only the roe deer unsuccessful.

The children visiting the Park, whether in school parties or with their parents, enjoyed feeding Sannox by hand. We would sell small bags of cattle nuts at the gate hut and he would wait, gently nuzzling and pestering the youngsters for the tasty cubes of dried food. The hind calves stayed in their enclosure, steadily maturing; they would not breed until their third summer at the earliest; I was planning for them to be sired by Sannox in due course.

However, approaching his second winter and now some fifteen months of age, Sannox suddenly started becoming very boisterous with everybody and everything around him. We could not risk any injury to visitors, so Sannox was introduced to the two Warnham hinds. However, if we thought that was the end to our problems, then we were mistaken. Sannox was blessed with an uncanny ability to negotiate 'red deer fencing'; perhaps it was a trait which he inherited from his parents and the wild herd that roamed on Arran.

His adventures were endless but the following episode is perhaps the one that summarises this roguish individual best.

I was dining in a Bristol steak house one autumn, 'red deer rut' time. Sannox was now fully mature and his first offspring were already browsing the woodland slopes. At around nine thirty, a uniformed policeman entered the restaurant and approached my table. In a quiet voice, he explained that at that moment Sannox, having discovered yet another way out of his enclosure, was terrorising a young couple. They were trapped in their mini van outside Ken's, the local fish and chip shop in Westbury-on-Trym.

"My colleagues are monitoring the situation closely," the officer continued, "but I feel, sir, you should make your way there as soon a possible to take control of the situation. We have a safety issue with customers using the 'chipper'."

Twenty minutes later I had arrived, having imagined several awful scenarios during my journey. The crowd which had gathered was silhouetted against the garish lights. I eased my way through the onlookers who were all staring in one direction, as if transfixed. I saw the parked mini van with the two people huddled together inside. Its headlights were smashed. At the same time, I spotted Sannox. He was next to the vehicle, standing absolutely still.

I hesitated; I was confused by what I was seeing.

Victoria Newman lived next door to the fish bar. A young horse rider of great potential and a long-time supporter of the Park, she had suffered a tragic accident; a helicopter en route to or from Bristol Filton aerodrome spooked her horse; in the ensuing accident, Vicki had suffered serious brain damage.

She had heard the commotion that night; whilst the police were tracking me, Vicki had collected a head collar and leading rein. She calmly walked up to Sannox as he battered the mini van. She spoke to him softly and although, so she told me later, he still had a wild stare about him and continued to roll his lips with flared nostrils, she gently dropped the head collar over his antlers. She retreated quietly, and two police officers moved forward to hold Sannox steady with the leading rein. She had performed brilliantly!

A few minutes later, having apologised and given my details to the couple in the mini van for the insurance claim that would surely follow, Vicki, the two policeman and I led Sannox back to his enclosure in the Park. The good news was that he was still there the next morning, peacefully feeding with the two adult Warnham hinds. Over the ensuing years, but always at 'rutting' time, he would often go absent again. Nevertheless, his excursions did diminish simply because the red deer enclosure increasingly resembled Fort Knox!

Maybe I took the wrong decision when I instantly accepted Sannox, but another 'spur of the moment' decision to a telephone call, this time from the Quantock Hills, was to prove fortuitous.

The request came from Dinhams, the coal merchants of Nether Stowey. A local farmer, cutting the first silage of the summer, had disturbed a red deer hind lying in long grass close to woodland. She had just calved and sat tight as the machinery came ever closer. At the very last moment, she had leapt to safety, but the blades caught the calf whose instinct had also been to stay absolutely still.

A local vet completed a clean amputation of the right foreleg at the shoulder; otherwise the calf was unharmed. She was bottle-fed by the farmer's wife and the golden labrador bitch kept her warm, licking and cleaning the stitched wound and being the 'foster mum', giving the calf the constant company which she required.

I don't remember now why 'Bambi' was returned to live free around the coal yard. However, this only proved practical for two or three months, for the young hind calf, now amazingly fleet of foot and without too recognisable a limp, began to stray ever further afield. Maybe it was just the call of the wild; more likely she craved the affections of the farmer's wife and the labrador, both which had clearly meant so much to her after the life-saving operation.

Bambi came to the Park; she was an instant hit. She could always be found idling, as if uninterested, close to the pony enclosure waiting for her special food. Bambi was stroked, youngsters were photographed with an arm around her neck, and occasionally, but always first thing in the morning, she would grab the whole bag instead of waiting to receive the food from the palm of a hand.

Sannox caused untold problems when in the rut; however, to be fair, he became an outstanding example of a mature Red deer stag.
© Jim Hale, 1972, courtesy Mia Hale

Occasionally, the cafe staff would need to make themselves scarce. A family would be sitting quietly enjoying their food and the surroundings. Bambi was never far away.

"D'ye know, I reckon that deer has only got three legs."

"Don't be stupid, that's impossible, it wouldn't walk like that."

"Well, it's standing still now and you tell me if you can see more than three. Go on, go and have a look for yourself."

There would be a pause as the person would stand next to Bambi, whilst putting a calming hand on her back and saying, "there, there," and at the same time leaning and peering all over her. Meanwhile, the cafe staff would stay just out of sight, listening closely.

"You're right you know, it has only got one front leg. Amazing, quite amazing. Aah, bless him. Or her! What is it, anyway?"

"Well, have another look."

"It looks like a 'her'," would come the response a while later. Then one of the family would go to the gate hut for yet another bag of deer food. Every member of staff had to know Bambi's life story and to also be prepared to make plenty of food bags. It was, though, a remarkable tale and she was a happy creature.

In the late 1960s, the 'country fox' was a common nocturnal hunter in the countryside surrounding Bristol.

But, there was another kind of fox whose numbers were rapidly increasing at that time, the 'town or urban fox'. They would be regularly seen abroad in daylight; there was soon the constant re-occurring problem of litters of cubs being found under sheds and log piles in city gardens, on allotments and in churchyards. When I was planning my lecture programme, I was keen to have hand-tame foxes and badgers to join the 'gang of four'. Finding some badger cubs could prove difficult and I would need some luck. However, with foxes, I reckoned I would have many opportunities.

"Do you realise we've been offered twenty-eight fox cubs just this last week?" my father mentioned at supper one evening.

"I know, and the staff are telling callers that we are unable to accept more; they are giving out the local RSPCA telephone number for further advice." There was another more telling reason for this response. A couple had rescued a cub the previous spring. She was now a striking and confident young vixen; having visited the Park they had decided that she would benefit by having more space and also be appreciated by so many more people. I found Rusty to be as tame as a dog; travelling, too, was no problem for her. I planned to spend many hours with her in close contact with youngsters in the classroom, and she quickly proved to be an absolute hit.

Within months Razzle, a more delicate vixen, and Nobby, a sturdy dog fox, had joined Rusty. All three were at ease together in a vehicle; all three could be handled by strangers, yet all three were very different characters, but each complimented the other. So, the three foxes would take everything, well almost everything, in their stride and could never be described as aggressive; they were gentle creatures without an ounce of vice between them.

I had been invited to present the annual Children's Lecture at Bristol University on a Saturday afternoon in late October before a capacity audience in a typical lecture theatre layout. The gang of four along with my foxes and badgers were the selected 'first team'.

My assistants were my close friends John and Judi Featherstone; thirty years later, John is one of the illustrators for *Face to Face,* his cartoons recapturing some humourous moments; Judi is godmother to our daughter Olivia, and I am godfather to their son Mark; our friendship has been lifelong. I was also being helped that afternoon by Helen, then my stunning girlfriend and, today, still my lovely wife, and also by Les Seaney, a close friend who had wanted for so long to be part of such an occasion. The four made up my 'support' team. All had gone well with much audience participation; now the youngsters eagerly awaited the arrival of the foxes.

Helen, Les and the Featherstones went to fetch the two foxes; I looked up as they entered from the back of the lecture theatre above me and saw Helen with Rusty and Les with Nobby. All the young-sters had turned towards them in expectation. The plan was for Helen and Les to carry both individuals to all four far corners of the theatre. I had no idea that Les was so nervous. Whether he was holding Nobby in a particularly uncomfortable way, or whether he was wearing an after-shave to which Nobby had taken an instant dislike, I shall never know. But, just before they came in, Nobby had

"Les – we're meant to be showing the youngsters NOBBY – not your BLOODY NOSE!"

www.cartoons4u.co.uk

bitten Les on the end of his nose, which was now bleeding profusely. The problem was that Les seemed to have switched off. His teeth were grit-ted and I was unable to make him hear or make any visual contact. I still have a clear memory of a face much resembling Tommy Cooper's when he said, 'not like that ... like that'.

The great challenge I received, in 1988, was from the long-running TV series, All Creatures Great And Small, for an episode to be filmed on location in Swaledale in the Yorkshire Dales, for Series Six. I had previ-ously written to the programme, telling them of my hand tame trio of foxes, mentioning that if a 'fox story' was to involve Siegfried Farnon, James Herriott and Calum Buchanan, the three partners in the fictional veterinary practice of Skeldale House,

106

I could not have wished for a more friendly trio of foxes, *Vulpes vulpes*, than vixens Rusty and Razzle and Nobby, a dog. Here is Razzle taking 'promotional' work in her stride.

then I was sure my animals would be ideal for the close-up footage, either on location or in the studio.

Helen and I were visited by two members of the team at our home, Tony Redston, Production Associate and Joy Lale, Script Editor. We promised that when they met the foxes for the first time, the latter would be in strange surroundings; so, we would, recreate one of the major hurdles of taking them away on location. Then, we invited them to sit with all three foxes together, whilst we discussed the logistics of the journey, their overnight quarters and the proposed sequences in the storyline. Needless to say, the foxes were a big hit!

The story would begin with Nobby being found unconscious in a country lane by Calum. He had been in a collision with a vehicle. Nobby, after being accurately weighed, had been sedated by Jack Watkinson, the programme's veterinary surgeon. Nobby was laid on a polystyrene mat on the hard surface of the lane. Calum was to come from the direction of Muker and, after braking hard to stop, would climb out of his ex US Army Jeep and kneel beside the still senseless Nobby. After examining him, he was to lift him gently into the vehicle before driving on.

After the usual three takes of every scene, we were disturbingly behind the planned time schedule. Finally, I was able to step in, collect Nobby, who was even now 'out to the world' and rush him to the surgery near Leyburn for the antidote to be administered. The vet was understandably disappointed at the delay and was concerned for Nobby's wellbeing. He was given the reversal agent and all I could do was to wait for Nobby to recover.

I returned to the location and, next, Calum was to be filmed close to the scene of Nobby's demise. He had returned to search for signs of an earth in current use, or even to spot

Rusty always seemed to know when I was fetching her for a journey. She would greet me with whimpering calls accompanied by her brush wagging. She loved company and meeting strangers.
© John and Tracy Langley, Chester, 2007
www.ourwildlifephotography.co.uk

another fox in the vicinity, maybe even the victim's mate. Razzle was to fulfil that role at long range. She was released into a lovely natural location, was completely steady over several minutes as ever increasing close-up shots were taken. So, this next stage was completed on schedule.

Meanwhile, I had heard disturbing news from the surgery. Nobby was not responding as expected. In layman's terms, he was still out for the count; I was concerned and expressed my fears. The vet decided to administer another stronger dose and asked one of the nurses to regularly monitor his heartbeat. By now it was six o'clock and Nobby had been in his other world for eight hours.

Meanwhile Razzle and Rusty waited anxiously for their friend. Two hours later, as I was understandably becoming ever more concerned, there was suddenly good news. Nobby was returning rapidly to full consciousness and, in no time, I was able to release him into the overnight accommodation; then I sat with all three of my close friends for a while. Much later, and well relieved, I had supper with the crew.

Next day, it was Rusty's turn for tight head shots and the story was coming together well. Nobby had rested well and was fully alert again. The big test would be the final sequences. Calum, in the storyline, was to release Nobby close to the wild foxes earth; the director wanted Nobby and one vixen meeting and acknowledging each other briefly as a wild pair of foxes might do on their territory. My concern was that both foxes would scurry off in different directions. However, everybody in the production team now knew that the foxes were hand tame, and so would be prepared to pick them up if they wandered out of shot; I simply couldn't be in half a dozen places at once! Unbelievably, when Nobby met Rusty, they greeted each other like long-lost friends. It was a fitting end to an emotive and touching storyline.

Whenever filming had been delayed for technical reasons, maybe the light was 'flat' or someone had started using a chainsaw in nearby woodland, the senior cameraman 'Laurie', was inevitably to be found talking fondly to, or stroking the foxes. Without doubt, he had taken a particular shine to Nobby; he was especially relieved to see him return after his immobilisation. When, finally, I left for home we shook hands; he said it had been a real pleasure getting to know the foxes and said "David, I hope we all meet again and sooner rather than later; perhaps, next time, it will be in the real world!"

Laurie was freelance; after the shooting for that All Creatures series throughout the Yorkshire Dales had concluded, he went to Africa to film a 'Jim'll Fix It' story. There, he contracted a strain of malaria against which his body failed to compete. Within three months of saying his fond farewells to Nobby, Laurie had lost his own life.

... by mid February badger cubs of all sizes would already be arriving ...

I had reckoned, correctly, that I would have little difficulty in acquiring hand-tame foxes, but handlable badgers might well prove to be a different proposition.

However, luck was again on my side. The Park was obtaining a high level of publicity in and around Bristol and badgers were a common mammal, particularly in the Cotswolds and the Forest of Dean. Inevitably, especially during the extensive building programmes throughout the 1960s, setts were being regularly disturbed and carelessly destroyed. Badgers breed early in the year, during February and March, and cubs of all sizes were being discovered.

I knew that I needed to hand rear sow cubs. From Norfolk days and from reading the experiences of the Black Country naturalist Phil Drabble, a hand-reared boar badger can easily turn nasty, biting with a vice-like grip, and inflicting painful wounds. I had witnessed such aggression. So, sow cubs it would be and, wherever possible, the boar cubs would be returned into the wild. We were very successful in rearing our cubs on Ostermilk No 2; they matured on a diet of minced meat, rolled oats, soaked biscuit

... members of my staff would diligently bottle-feed ...

meal with occasional 'left-over' cooked vegetables, yeast and raw eggs.

An early Collins 'New Naturalist' publication entitled *The Badger*, had been written by Dr. Ernest Neal. A lifelong authority on these nocturnal mammals, we had become close friends when I served alongside him as a Council Member of the Somerset Trust for Nature Conservation. One of his researchers was Dr. Chris Cheeseman; he was carrying out long-term studies of badger behaviour and their breeding successes in setts on the Cotswolds. Now, with much of the original data amended, a revamped edition of Neal's monograph was published. The review was recorded in a stable in the Park with Neal, Cheeseman and myself,

... with the end result that, probably, I had the three tamest sow badgers nationwide during the '70s and '80s.
all photographs © Jim Hale, courtesy Mia Hale

the interviewer and sound recordist and all the necessary equipment, plus the closest of attentions from three tame sow badgers.

As the years passed I did accumulate too many badgers; it was difficult to turn away some youngsters given the circumstances in which they were offered. They were tame but lived in a semi-feral group. However, my 'lecture' characters were kept separate and, easily accessible, were handled in front of visitors nearly every day.

An unexpected lifeline resolved a difficult situation. Professor Hans Kruuk of the Terrestrial Research Unit, now the Centre for Ecology and Hydrology at Banchory, was commencing research on the spatial relationships of a family group of badgers. Special observation huts were constructed and, through a strengthened glass floor, he was able to watch the close contact behaviour of several badgers in the artificial sett below. He wanted to understand how and when, and if possible why, breeding sows gather together with non-breeding sows or 'aunties', with young sows remaining close by on the periphery. For this group, one boar badger would dominate. Meanwhile, less dominant or younger boars, almost understudies, will live in loose homosexual groups in adjacent artificial setts. Kruuk planned to observe the selection process between the various boars, one of which will eventually come forward to challenge the 'boar in residence'; most of this selection process, of course, takes place below ground in the wild; at Aboyne, Kruuk could study unobserved. To ease identification he planned to regularly colour mark the group of some ten individuals that Helen and I transported; being tame, re-catching them for re-marking would prove easy so, at no time, would they become stressed.

I was thrilled to subsequently hear that the sows were soon breeding. All our efforts to successfully hand-rear them to maturity at different times had been rewarded. The extended group were happy together and provided much new and important knowledge

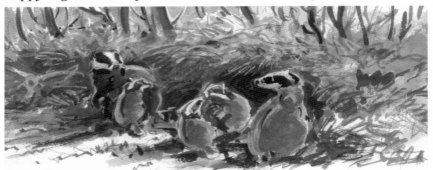

Hans Kruuk, at Aboyne, studied individual relationships within their family group; Gerald Durrell, for *The Amateur Naturalist*, wanted to recapture this typical woodland scene by filming with my hand-tame trio of badgers.

Personal friends Bill and Grace Natzger spent hours broadening horizons; here is Grace with Ulla, one of my alsatians, doing just that!
© Bill Natzger, 1974

about their wild cousins' complicated family lives underground.

My hand-tame sows were gaining a reputation. Even in strange conditions, they would remain unnerved; indeed, I was confident to allow complete strangers to handle them, particularly a sow called Morag. They were filmed many times on location by well-known cameramen and production teams. Each time the call came I had that jump of excitement and expectation that came with the fresh challenge, as when BAFTA winning cameraman, Maurice Tibbles tracked them under floodlight on the lawns of Lord Bath's Longleat House, in Wiltshire. However, one request was special, and, frankly, the questions took me aback.

"Would you be prepared to risk your badgers close to active setts? It would be for the Amateur Naturalist. You know the book by Gerald Durrell, do you? Filming would be on the Lydney Park Estate, courtesy of Lord Bledisloe. Durrell will be doing the voice-overs live to camera. We would be delighted to see you and your badgers. Could we discuss the potential problems you might foresee as soon as possible?" The queries came thick and fast.

I arrived at the location in mid-afternoon. Quietly, I approached the woodland where the tell-tale signs of extensive badger occupation were obvious. The cameras were already in position next to two well-used setts. The spoil heaps of used bedding had clearly been dragged out over a long period of time by the occupants.

The producer introduced me to Lee Durrell, but Gerald

An all-embracing upbringing meant that my sow badgers, especially Morag, were always calm, even in the most artificial situations.

Durrell was, at that moment, gently snoozing in the director's chair; he had just finished lunch! I met the camera and sound crews and then we looked in detail at exactly where I might release the badgers.

Tame as my trio were, all badgers are mighty strong; the Welsh or Celtic word is *mochyn daear* which roughly translated means 'earth pig'. They are animals that are best compared to a rugby prop forward; both have a low centre of gravity and no neck! They can dig under, and out of, anywhere. So, the next hour was spent tightly rolling several lengths of wire netting and securing them, and I really do mean securing them, at a good arm's length inside the entrance tunnels; it was important that the wire could not be seen whilst filming, and secondly, I would need to place a badger 'out of sight' so it could be filmed 'leaving' the sett. Everything had to be absolutely secure, we could not risk losing an animal. We laid blankets so as not to disturb the ground and were careful not to damage the vegetation, as we discreetly hid morsels of cat food and the occasional slither cut from a Mars Bar. My animals were very tame and were completely unfazed by events, never stirring even when strangers took a close look at them in their travelling crate. We planned to go straight into 'live' takes; if Gerald Durrell could simultaneously complete his voice-over we could swiftly move through the sequences.

During the afternoon, the light levels improved and by five o'clock the edge of the woodland glade was bathed in a soft evening light. Gerald Durrell had met the badgers and was quietly rehearsing his scripts, concentrating on the descriptive passages he would put to camera with the consummate ease of a well-informed naturalist and in his own inimitable style.

Suddenly, we were on! Everybody was fascinated by the sows' behaviour; they did exactly what was required, long shots, close ups, exploring and exiting the setts, with the occasional spontaneity of a snout catching a strange scent on the breeze, or a raised foreleg tantalisingly but briefly held, just like wild badgers; they were faultless.

The director went for broke on the final sequence. The badgers were released again and this time Durrell was sitting even closer. He recorded almost the same narrative, word for word, with one of the trio always, it seemed, within both ear and eye shot!

These were some of the best planned and most natural shots I had ever achieved. My privilege was to share them with one of the outstanding naturalists of the 20th century. Scott, Lockley and Durrell were and still are my heroes; each possessed certain qualities, an inner truth, rarely found since in other naturalists. Each had very different personalities, but all three contributed and shared a lifetime's commitment to the same cause. Each was searching for ever more knowledge on their subject, however mundane the source, which they always shared with sincerity and without hesitation or prejudice to listening, watching and reading audiences. Each embraced Gilbert White's great chain of nature; "curiosity, passion and enthusiasm." Finally, they also knew what role, and at what level of priority, wildlife conservation and the quality of the natural world across the planet should play in the everyday lives of both nations and individuals. There have been very few better since Peter Scott, Ronald Lockley and Gerald Durrell. Our unique planet earth, you and I, owe them an immeasurable gratitude.

Chapter Seven

"The bitch has just had twins. An unbelievable experience!"

British Otter; *lutra lutra*
© John Threlfall 2007
www.johnthrelfall.co.uk

"The otter population is coming back strongly now, but it is coming back into a different world. Regard for the species with the public is much better than ever it was and it is essential to keep it that way."

Dr Don Jefferies, English Nature, 2001

Since 1988, there has been evidence of significant infectious diseases in otters. Since 2004, however, post mortem examinations have revealed severe thickening and fibrosis of the gall bladder, with lesions due to a bile fluke, a parasite common in Eastern Europe. The import of topmouth gudgeon and sunbleak via an aquarist centre in southern England, followed by their escape, has led to the latter colonising the Somerset Levels in the 1990s. Following the most recent diagnoses, it is now known that the infection is established in Somerset, parts of Dorset and also, worryingly, in East Anglia. Jefferies' comments of 2001 (above) well illustrate the importance of the need for ongoing health monitoring of the UK otter population.

source: Veterinary Record (2005) 157, 49-52.
V R Simpson BVSc, DTVM, FIBiol, Hon FRCVS, Wildlife Veterinary Investigation Centre, Truro, Cornwall

You take my house when you do take the prop
That doth sustain my house; you take my life
When you do take the means whereby I live

Shakespeare
The Merchant of Venice

On Islay a female brings her cubs
onto the edge of the sea lochs
to feed. On the rocks are Dunlin
& Turnstones, still in breeding plumage.

Two Great Skua's pass
mobbed by a Hooded C

Loch Gruinart, Islay
In the distance the Paps of
Jura still have snow on them.

She is teaching the
youngsters to hunt among
the rocks & kelp for
crabs & fish.

The Eiders are busy
displaying to each
other. One drake is
throwing his head back
& calling to a female

The missing cub spots its
mother & sibling & swims
towards them.

STEVE CALE
2007

"Where do you think you're going to get a tank of petrol on today of all days?" was my mother's first response to a telephone call that I had just taken from Bob Cooke.

Bob and I had become close friends during the two summers I had worked in north Norfolk with the naturalist Philip Wayre. I had been introduced to Bob and his wife Joan after a chance encounter with Brent Pope, when the latter had called to the Wayres' home hoping to buy some young wildfowl for his collection. Brent's parents then owned the Manor Hotel in Blakeney, and some of the marshes that make up the magical north Norfolk coast between Cley-next-the-Sea and Salthouse.

Bob, an auxiliary coastguard, had for a long time been a man of these wild coastal marshes, guiding visitors to its secret places to discover the special wildlife species. In spring and summer he knew, out of the back of his hand, the narrow and concealed pathways amongst the reedbeds; at the same time, he did not disturb the farmer's stock of store cattle that gently grazed these rich summer meadows. The species that are so difficult to spot from a distance were the birds with which he could make close contact; amongst the sedge and phragmites beds he treated you to stunning views of bearded tits, reed and sedge warblers, reed buntings, garganey teal and the ever shy water rails. With luck, too, and by making use of the reedbeds as they decayed, and some of which would have been

The rapid shrinkage of wetlands and estuaries is a worldwide problem; half of the world's original wetlands have been destroyed or have disappeared since 1990. Wetlands play an essential part in otters' lives, yet they also play a central part in human communities by controlling flooding and preserving our drinking water supplies.
source: Earth from the Air, a photographic portrait of our planet, Yann Arthus-Bertrand, 2006

left deliberately uncut to provide cover, you could close in with him for close encounters with lapwing, snipe, redshank, greenshank and that wide variety of small 'grey' or 'brown' waders which pass through on autumn or spring passage. Here, they roosted on the sodden pastures, particularly during those periods when the tides cover their food rich tidal mudflats nearby, or when sheltering from the worst of the cold north Arctic-borne winds. Then the stunning close-ups were of wigeon, teal, and his long-time favourites, the dark-bellied Brent geese.

Bob knew of my plans for the Wildlife Park when I came down from Cambridge. During my time at university I had been a frequent visitor to the Manor House, his home which lay close to the coast road. At the end of my last Christmas term, I had walked the marsh track to the shingle ridge that protected the meadows and reed-fringed drainage ditches from the worst ravages of the North Sea. At the top of the ridge I had, literally, leant forward at forty-five degrees into the teeth of the howling gale; the noise was unbelievable with the sound of the waves pounding onto the beach, immediately accompanied by the roar of the receding shingle, before yet again, the next breaker swept in; it was a frightening place to be.

It was cold too, unbelievably cold that night in the pitch darkness. I was glad to reach the warmth of the Cookes' upstairs lounge, upstairs because in the disaster of the East Coast flood surge of 1953, the ground floor had been flooded to a depth of several feet. The high water mark recorded on the front porch is at a staggering height. Bacon butties and mugs of tea, whilst sat alongside the incessantly chattering mynah bird, and, simultaneously, snuggling the springer spaniel in my lap, was just the welcome needed that wild winter's night.

Tiki, my first otter, is looking for me through the door of her enclosure. She had been 'fetched' off wet mud on an ebbing tide on Salthouse Marsh, north Norfolk, on Boxing Day morning 1966
© Jim Hale, 1967, courtesy Mia Hale

One year later, Bob's telephone call on Boxing Day 1966, had confirmed that earlier that morning, and while out on coastguard watch he had put Judy, his springer bitch, onto the wet mud left by an ebbing tide. She had successfully 'fetched' a stranded otter cub.

Bob had told me about two bitch otters that frequented the marshes; one defined and marked her territory by regularly sprainting in the ditches and reedbeds close to Salthouse; the other's favourite patch was a couple of miles away, somewhere alongside the water meadows of the River Glaven, which exits to the sea under the main road to and from Blakeney. The dog would visit both in turn; the bitches would be on heat every forty-five days, with any subsequent pregnancy lasting sixty-three days. I had been on the marshes several times with Bob, but we had never caught sight of either individual, yet I had seen very fresh spraint at different locations which Bob knew the Salthouse bitch favoured. I remember, too, that I never did see an otter with Frank Owen either on the upland bog of Tregaron.

She was never happier than when exploring, especially in wintertime
© Jim Hale, 1967, courtesy Mia Hale

"Can you come today, now, this afternoon? The cub is quite well grown, probably just starting to feed for itself. We'll stay up late for you tonight. Telephone us as you leave, if you're coming." He sounded anxious.

My mother's remark had immediately summed up our problem. Where could we possibly get enough fuel for the journey? Straightaway, my father was on the phone; we hit lucky with the first call. We lived close to Clifton village; my father's architect's practice and my mother's two hairdressing salons were well established businesses within the local community. Another similar 'family' business was the local garage, providing fuel, repairs and coaches for hire. It was jointly owned and run by four brothers, the Kear family. I had been at school at nearby Clifton College and it was 'Kears' coaches that took the cricket and rugger teams on many of their away trips. One of the brothers generously agreed to leave his family's festivities. Within half an hour I had

I have seen fresh spraint both on Salthouse Marsh and on the Tregaron Bog, but have yet to see a wild otter at either place.
© Ian Anderson, Somerset 1980.

returned home, ready to leave for the north Norfolk coast with a filled tank and a couple of full spare cans.

I described in detail the journey that Christmastime and subsequent events in *Stormforce an otter's tale.* But since recording that experience nearly ten years ago, I have reflected further.

The drive across England will always be clearly etched in my mind; I can still sense the ever-increasing strength of the gale, particularly when I had passed my old university town and headed towards the flat lands of East Anglia.

I remember the growing feeling of intense excitement as I closed on my destination; it was approaching midnight as I descended the Glaven valley from Holt and the suspense was alarming. Within minutes, I would see an otter cub for the first time; I had no idea whatsoever then that it was going to be the first of many otters and like Storm, also born to a wild mother, would engulf both my and my family's lives over the ensuing thirty-five years.

As I turned onto the Cley and Salthouse coast road, I met the gale head on; and those moments that December night on the shingle ridge are now vivid in my mind again; I felt relief as I swept into the steep forecourt of the Cookes' home and was instantly relieved as the lights brightened in the porch.

Within minutes I was staring at a tiny creature, which was absolutely beguiling; she was snug, curled up asleep, and safe now, enveloped in one of Bob's close-knit woollen sweaters. However, she was unaware she was to be the start of a whole new era in my life. I called her Tiki, for otters are great wanderers and shy of man.

Fifteen years later, and very late at night, I had been sitting for a long time by an artificial holt in the midst of my collection of otters,

... Otters, particularly bitch otters, have dominated both my and my family's lives over thirty five years ...
© Nick Martin, www.martinimages.co.uk

watching one bitch closely. I wanted so much to become only the second person to breed the British otter in the UK in the past hundred years. My friend, Philip Wayre, had begun to breed otters in some numbers and was planning, with the co-operation of the then Nature Conservancy Council and by meeting their exact criteria, to release unrelated trios of parent-reared cubs into the waterways of eastern England, and from which they had completely disappeared.

Dr Don Jefferies, specialising in otters, the late Dr Derek Ratcliffe whose special interest was peregrine falcons and Dr David Bellamy researching as a botanist, were among a group of scientists advising the Government from the Monks Wood Research Station. They were arguing strongly against the proposed use of organo-chlorine weedkillers and insecticides. Nevertheless, Dieldrin, Aldrin and

This could be a photograph of either Cider or his offspring Blackthorn, which were two of the finest dog otters in my collection. Ted Hughes wrote: otters have 'a round head like an old tomcat...'
© Ross Hoddinott. www.rosshoddinott.co.uk

Lindane were introduced, during '56 and '57, throughout the arable farming areas of southern and eastern England and in the sheep dips of the traditional sheep-rearing hill country, mainly found in northern and western parts of the UK. The scientists' expertise and recommendations were ignored by the civil servants and politicians.

"There are those in life who go out and do, and there are those who can't. However, many of the latter then spend most of their time telling others what to do," words told to me by Geoff Doran, veterinary surgeon to my Wildlife Park. A true Yorkshireman, he had been recommended by another vet and family friend, Manson Baird, as being the right person to cope with the great variety of animals and birds that would eventually be in my care. Geoff Doran always spoke directly and truthfully; at my first meeting, having read my letter of introduction, he looked me straight in the eye and said, "it will be a pleasure to be your vet as long as you will accept one condition; that we will win some and lose some; on that condition it will be a pleasure to accept the challenge to be the vet to your Wildlife Park." The late Geoff Doran never let me down.

Many politicians then, and many more of them now, fell into that category of telling others what to do; the scientists' advice was totally ignored; diurnal and noctural hunters, peregrine falcons and barn owls, both at the head of a food chain, were soon in trouble. Herons at the head of a wetland food chain similarly suffered; otters were

After the introduction of organo-chlorines in '56 and '57, many species at the head of their food chains were soon in trouble; the peregrine falcon, *Falco peregrinus*, was a prime example.
© John and Tracy Langley, Chester
www.ourwildlifephotography.co.uk

devastated; the level of chemical residues discovered in the fatty tissues of eels, which are the otter's favourite food, had to be seen to be believed. The first National Otter Survey in 1978 showed that twenty years after the introduction of the organo-chlorines, less than one hundred otters were left alive in England. Well done the politicians!

But how many more times could we say that, and not just about wildlife issues? The list would, indeed, be endless.

I thought my calculations might be right. I had observed earlier, through spy holes in the interwoven fencing surrounding the pens, my bitch otter mating with her dog on a couple of occasions. By moving unobtrusively and always leaving water gently running into their tanks to create a settling background noise, the otters were unaware of my presence. It was Bob Cooke who suggested creating as natural an environment as possible to help his Salthouse cub to settle and feed. It proved a success. Unseen, I could watch the animals at play, play which would often lead to spontaneous courtship. But courtship did not necessarily lead to mating; the dog would frequently be too aggressive; the bitch, on heat every forty-five days, would only need to couple with the dog on just two occasions; she could become nervous and would resort to being ever more aggressive to keep a persistent dog at distance. Then it was important to be able to watch both participants carefully; my enclosures were constructed so that I could always easily separate the dog into an adjacent pen. I grew to know the sounds of real affection, the chatter, the intimate small talk so different, so much softer than during much of their foreplay. Late at night and into the early hours, and still not that far from the enclosures, I would continue to distinguish the tell-tale sounds of their activities. By recording the dates of potential successful matings, I had a good idea, given a sixty-three day pregnancy, of when a bitch might give birth.

This was now my third night of waiting, and surely I would have success this time; if not, then maybe I was 'pairing' her with the wrong dog. The artificial holt was, in fact, a long rectangular box; with bales of straw on three sides and on the top. The bitch had created a single entrance tunnel through the bedding; even if I shone a bright light, she would remain relaxed as she gently raised her head. She would continue to look at me before twisting and curling in on herself to sleep further. Always available was a dish of fresh food, diced chunks of ox heart, liver and some slivers of silver eel. A small galvanised tank was always full of fresh water and was regularly being refilled. At just past midnight the surface was flaky, it was that cold!.

"I thought my calculation would be right ... this was now my third night of waiting..."

In the absolute silence, I suddenly but briefly heard a distinct sound, a faint squeaking cry. Was I dreaming this delicate noise?

120

I waited, for how long I cannot recall, but some time later I heard it again. Something else was alive in there; surely it was my first otter cub.

Philip Wayre had taught me much, very often through brief, almost throw-away, remarks. I remember one, often repeated which was 'leave well alone.' Another when an abandoned or orphaned creature would arrive, or a

My first otter cub was reared during the winter of '80 and '81.

rare bird or animal was born, was when he would remind me of the three critical periods of survival, "three days, three weeks, and often just when you think you are home and dry, three months." It is uncanny how many times he was proven correct over the years.

However, inevitably, my anxiety and curiosity got the better of me

'More meat than fish'; my otters and their cubs had regular and ample portions of ox heart, liver, whiting, and whenever possible, silver eel.

in the early hours. I reckoned if I shone the torch just one more time, the bitch would twist and turn and I would possibly hear the cub again. Reason and common sense had just gone out of the window! I switched on the beam. The bitch, no more than four feet away, stared at me; she turned and curled like the cat that sits on your lap. Immediately, there were more spontaneous and similar cries.

My first otter cub was reared by its mother during the winter of '80 and '81. I had become only the second person to Philip Wayre to successfully breed the British otter in a collection in the last hundred years. Subsequently, some thirty-five offspring were parent reared in my collection over the next twenty-five years, and I was pleased to be able to donate many youngsters to the Otter Trust. They contributed to Philip and Jeanne Wayre's ground-breaking and innovative programme of releasing trios of youngsters into areas from which their wild cousins had disappeared. Most of this programme, meeting all the standards requested by the Nature Conservancy Council, then English Nature, and now Natural England, was carried out in the arable eastern counties of England. The released animals bred; in turn, their cubs became successful parents, and

I had become only the second person to breed the British Otter in a collection in the last hundred years

photographs pp 120 & 121
© and courtesy Ian Anderson, 1980

121

now the otter is clearly but slowly becoming re-established through-out the Fens, the Broads, the rest of eastern England and beyond.

Every otter hides a different character, like children, like English springer spaniels, even when twin brothers or sisters and younger siblings are born to the same mother over successive years.

Tigger was a dominant and aggressive dog but never fathered any cubs whereas Cider, quietly strong and assertive, bred with every bitch which I ran with him. Blackthorn, his son, was a 'chip off the old block', and sired many progeny particularly with Pebble and Ripple, the last two adult bitches in my collection.

I found over the years that the slighter, feistier bitches were more likely to breed; it was strange, too, that when one bitch started breeding, another would as well. A year or eighteen months would then pass with no births, only for breeding to start once again. Rowan and Houdini were two prolific mothers; Rowan dropped triplets prematurely on one occasion and, as a last resort, I used a hairdryer to try and revive them in order to bottle feed them, alas to no avail. The cubs were full term weighing seventy-eight grams, I fully expected Houdini to have her litter within forty-eight hours. She never cubbed or, did she, in fact? She was as wild as Rowan was tame; she could have similarly aborted and I would never have known, being unable to get close to her to collect any lifeless young-sters. However, within another three months, having run with their respective dogs at the due time, both bitches cubbed twins, the usual number, almost simultaneously. Both sets of twins survived.

The twin sisters Islay and Jura were different again; Islay brought many cubs to maturity over five or six years but Jura never cubbed; she was kept under the same conditions, had the same diet and was put to both the same and different dogs, all to no avail.

Willow was my most pro-lific bitch otter; after a rela-tively inauspicious start with a single but rather beautiful bitch cub, she continued at intervals of every twelve to fifteen months, with firstly twins, then triplets and

Stillborn twin cubs, full term, after a pregnancy of 63 days, and weighing 78 grams.

finally quads. All came through to full maturity. I have described listening for the tell-tale cries of new-born cubs, so I knew that Willow had at least twin cubs as she cubbed for the fourth time. It was impossible to say that there were three cubs from faint sounds,

122

but clearly I was hoping for triplets a second time. After the first very brief period of cub communication, everything goes quiet; I would have to wait, for at least five or six weeks, for the first cub or cubs to follow their mother out of the holt as she encouraged them to emerge and start taking solid food. I was delighted when I regularly confirm

On their territory, a bitch otter is an elusive creature, shy of man.
courtesy of John and Mandy Allen, Tamar Otter and Wildlife Centre, North Petherwin, Cornwall.

three again, but during the afternoon feed when, unbelievably, I identified a fourth cub, well, it was a very special moment indeed; British otters can only give birth to a maximum of four cubs.

Over twenty-five years I developed the ability to track my otters closely without their knowledge; I was able to enter their private and personal lives. All loved to play beneath a hose, which splashed fresh water continually into their tanks; always fresh and clean, the tanks were emptied and refilled every day, so reminiscent of my efforts with the seals in the Wildlife Park. By providing the best of food and frequently changing their deep and soft beds of loose straw, I gave them a real stimulus to their everyday lives. For the most part they lived apart exactly reciprocating their wild relations; two bitches lived either side of a dog, with one cohabiting when appropriate; his access and departure was through the lobby and inter-connecting doors. When a bitch had given birth, I had an accurate understanding of her body's cycle. Such close attention to detail was instilled during my tutorship with Philip Wayre. I could recognise the otter's equivalent to morning sickness; I knew when the bitches had taken to lying up and, then, that rest, no disturbance and regular food full of protein, were as necessary as with any pregnant woman. In the final days, the bitches would float upside down in their tanks, just occasionally rolling in the clean water. Forty-eight hours before a birth I could see, when the fur was wet, little twin 'torpedoes', the outlines of the foetuses at the bottom of the stomach, before they passed into the uterus, the hollow muscular organ lying within the pelvic cavity of the bitch, and their eventual birth.

So, over thirty-five years I have intimately enjoyed a succession of otters; a similar number of cubs were reared by their mothers with one significant exception. I have studied their intimate behaviour on an almost daily basis. Nevertheless, and although so close to them, I never witnessed, to my regret, a bitch giving birth. That good fortune fell to an artist and personal friend, the late John Cooksley.

John was a secondary school teacher in Taunton he lived with his family in the Quantocks. We had met at one of my lectures and soon he was visiting our home in north Somerset to sketch our family of otters at close quarters.

One Saturday lunchtime, as I was leaving to support a charity lunch at my nearby church, John unexpectedly pulled alongside on his motorbike.

Twin bitch cubs which were bred in my collection; both became prolific mothers ... yet Houdini (top) was as wild as Rowan was tame ...
© Ian Anderson, Somerset, 1984

"Just thought I might be able to put in some time sketching the otters, if possible. Sorry, I forgot to ring you. Is it inconvenient? You're going out, aren't you?"

"No problem, help yourself," I replied. "I'll tell you where the keys are and you let yourself in wherever you want to go. Just one thing though. Don't forget to put the keys back, I'll be in a right mess without them. So see you again soon."

With that we parted company. A few hours later I went to the small preparation room to prepare the evening feeds. The keys were on the hook, fine; there was a folded piece of paper on a chopping board, with a knife lying across it. Just a note of thanks, I thought as, rather absent-mindedly, I unfolded it.

It read: *'Thought you should know that the bitch in the third pen had twin cubs this afternoon; I watched the whole thing but she's now hidden them in the bedding. I couldn't see anything when I left. Didn't draw, just stayed still, and she took no notice at all. It was an unbelievable experience! Will ring, thanks, John.'*

John would complete the most sensitive of work; he was so talented he was able to leave his teaching career and fulfill his dream of becoming a full-time artist. His delicate pencil drawings of my otters 'front' each chapter in *Stormforce, an otter's tale*. I still mourn his sudden and premature passing which was, sadly, before he saw his sketches in print.

My wife, Helen, answered a telephone call in mid-February 1992 and after the opening exchanges said, 'are you sure it's not a mink?' It was not the first time those words had been said to the caller. After several attempts Francesca Burrows was tired of what, to her, appeared to be deliberate evasive responses. Helen was not stalling. In fact, we regularly received calls from all over the south-west from people who had seen an otter, had an otter on their lawn or in their garden shed, or had seen one dead by the roadside. Questions covering size and colour, especially when the answer to the latter was black, meant that the caller had, no doubt, spotted a mink.

Helen's immediate response, however, to Francesca's description of the tiny bundle she was at that moment trying to encourage to suckle, was decisive. Francesca's husband, Graham, had over twenty-four hours previously picked up a tiny creature in a remote lane on Exmoor. He kept a private collection of hawks and owls and always had a 'bunny bag' in his Post Office van for the casualties of the night. When he had stopped on this occasion before first light on a wild February morning, it was no quarter-grown rabbit. It was an otter cub, weighing just one pound seven ounces and still alive.

"David will come this afternoon. I'll ring him immediately. I'll ask him to press on with feeding our collection. I'm sure he'll be there as soon as possible. I'll take directions if I may."

That journey and eventually collecting only my second wild and abandoned otter cub is told in detail in *Stormforce, an otter's tale*. Now, as I summarise half a lifetime spent with otters, I describe an event that occurred nearly every day of that Storm's adult life. It will provide the reader with an insight into the very essence of the relationship which I built with this remarkable wild creature.

Late, after the ITN national news, I would spend time with Storm in her enclosure which was always lit at night. I would first see her through a large window as I approached from indoors; she would be playing excitedly, plunging dolphin-style in her tank. Her time clock had kicked in and she was already expressing her excited and fun greeting. As I passed her on my way into her 'inner' den, she would jump out onto a straw bale, shimmer, sending droplets of water everywhere, glance at me briefly, then dive back into the pool to continue playing. Her den, originally a standard ten by ten garden shed, had been upgraded and customised. It formed one corner of her enclosure. Inside, was one of her travelling crates where she would sleep. My chair was alongside and her coarse dark green 'Wimbledon' towel lay stretched over the top. There was mains electricity, too, for general lighting and in case of the need for the warmth from an infra-red lamp.

I would leave her bowl of food, and sit down with a clipboard, paper and pen. I would commence answering my correspondence. After a while, Storm would come as far as the threshold of the door and shimmer yet again, thus losing the excess water from the fine outer guard hairs of her coat. Next, she would either spraint and or urinate on a heavy-duty and ridged rubber mat, redefining her personal territory for the umpteenth time. She would pad across the floor and spring, in two consecutive movements, firstly onto my lap and then again, after only momentarily hesitating, past my shoulder onto the towel on top of her crate. There, she would wriggle and squirm making sure every possible part of her body was nearly dry. The Oxford English Dictionary's definition of a contortionist is: *a performer who bends or twists out of place or shape his or her body for the entertainment of others.* That was Storm, in a nutshell!

A while later, Storm would be sniffing and nudging me around the back of my neck; she would nibble an ear and sometimes that hurt; then she would push her head and shoulders inside the collar of my smock or shirt, at first at the back of my neck and then into my open neck, all to no avail. Eventually, she would give up and peer into my face. It was almost as if she was telling me that she now wanted to curl up on my lap. Once she was settled, I

Storm would be content to stay close, held against my smock for long periods of time.
© Keith Savory, Edingworth, North Somerset, 1995

would gently lay the clipboard on her and continue writing again. Presently, she would go to sleep. Occasionally, she would twist and turn, all the time becoming ever more upside down; all I needed to do was to gently lift the clipboard every time I felt her move.

We would stay together for a long while; it could be well past midnight with my sleep beckoning before I would gently slide Storm to the floor and make my exit. Inevitably, my last sight of her was of her tucking into her favourite morsels; she always ate the portion of liver first. Minutes later, as I made my way upstairs, I would take one last look into her enclosure; she would be playing again, performing her favourite tumble turns; I would switch off the lights, but I would still be hearing her when I lost consciousness.

I knew many otters very well; my intimate relationship with Storm, born to a wild mother, a kinship shared over the best part of a decade was certainly one of the defining experiences of my life. Otters, whether they are Giant Brazilians in the Amazon, Short-clawed in the Mekong Delta or the Pacific Sea otters of the kelp beds off California, must survive. The wild places where they all live, in this country and throughout other wetland and marine enviornments worldwide, must endure too. They are presently severly threatened. Are we all prepared to change our lifestyles enough to ensure the future survival of otters and their wild natural homes?

I apologise if I have found it hard to define the otter even though I knew Storm so well. I commend you now to read the Poet Laureate,

the late Ted Hughes' poem, 'The Otter'. He generously allowed me to use it as the foreword to *Stormforce, an otter's tale*. The first words give us a most evocative yet accurate description of these mammals.

No story about otters is complete without this photograph. This is Sian, close to the Trotternish Isles, off the northern shores of Islay.
© Nick Gordon, Islay, 1996
... underwater eyes, an eel's oil of water body ...
© and courtesy the late Ted Hughes, the Poet Laureate.

'underwater eyes, an eel's oil of water body, neither fish nor beast is the otter.'

Gavin Maxwell in *Ring of Bright Water* wrote, *'it's no will-o-the-wisp that I have followed here;* the Oxford English Dictionary definition of 'will-o-the-wisp' is: *'an animal that is elusive and allures and misleads ...'*

Go to the north Norfolk coast, Morston, Stiffkey, Cley and in particular Salthouse, where Bob lived; journey to the Inner Hebrides and to the islands of Islay and Mull, the latter was where my dear friend, wildlife cameraman Nick Gordon, had made his home before his untimely and sudden death, whilst filming in the upper reaches of the Amazon Basin. Finally, explore the valley of the River Teifi and, in particular, the peat wilderness and raised bog of Cors Caron.

All of these are contrasting areas in the UK where the elusive otter can be seen; but they are places, too, where if you are lucky to see an individual, albeit only fleetingly, the nearby scenery will add extra dimension to an already enduring experience.

When I was fifteen, Frank Owen, keeper for the Tregaron Bog and the Teifi Pools, explained to me how the dog

... the dog otter will have a favourite couch amongst the more remote expanses of cottongrass ...

otter would have his favourite couches way out amongst the more remote expanses of purple moor grass, sedges and cottongrass. The bitch otters would anchor their respective territories away from the main marsh. Their preferred places would be within quick and easy access to fresh flowing water. Cover was vital for them too, in reedbeds and the adjacent dense dwarf shrub and bush thickets, where the bitches would establish both their permanent and transitory holts.

Frank had stressed how good sources of protein were vital for the bitch otter; silver eels, an otter's favourite food, would provide that, but another supply would come from preying on quarter-grown rabbits. So the bitch could well establish a holt with a rabbit warren close by, and where there would be, therefore, easy pickings of young kits in most months of the year.

I did visit one regularly used holt with Frank on several occasions. Without fail, we always spotted fresh spraint; this bitch was elusive but I always felt that she was never that far away from us; she was probably watching us as we were looking for her!

I stopped alongside the Bog many years later. It was when Elizabeth, Frank's widow, was still at 'Pontry'. I waited, allowing my bitch alsatian, Tina, to stretch her legs, and looked out for a while across the Bog. There were flocks of wigeon and teal nearby. I listened to the drake wigeon whistling, they were already courting their favoured ducks. A few redwings and fieldfares had arrived ahead of a cold snap in the weather and were feeding 'hard' as is their nature; a couple of red kites were finally on their way to roost in one of the oakwoods on the valley side.

There is something about the wildness of this place; you immediately think of otters and I clearly heard them before I left the wilderness. By the early 1980s, I had my own breeding pairs and the sounds I heard at dusk that evening and which I recall now, were clearly the emotive and affectionate chatter prior to a dog and bitch otter mating. I wasn't that far from Maesllyn Cottage and Frank's favourite otter holt!

The 2006 noticeboard in the Red Kite Centre in Tregaron records otters being sighted on several occasions on the freshwater pool not a quarter of a mile from the Owens' steading. However, I have yet to see an otter anywhere on the river Teifi from its source in the hills to the north east above Tregaron, to where its waters eventually empty to the west downstream of Aberteifi into the great sweep of Cardigan Bay, between Gwbert-on-Sea and Poppit Sands.

Wild otters are very, very elusive creatures; concentrate your efforts when looking for them over the couple of hours either side of high water, regardless of the time of day or night, for that's when fish are on the move. Here's a tip; purchase your local tide timetable and I hope you will have better fortune than Helen and I. Write and tell me if you are successful, it would be good to hear from you.

Good luck! Whatever, it will be well worth waiting for, I promise.

Chapter Eight

Beyond my wildest dreams ...

Barn Owl, *Tyto alba*
© John Threlfall 2007
www.johnthrelfall.co.uk

Owl is my favourite
Who flies like a nothing in the night, who whoing.
Is a feather duster in leafy corners
Ring a rosying boles of mice,
Twice you hear him call,
Who is he looking for
As he hoovers over the floor of the wood.

The principle of surprise is vital for predators. A precise sense both of vision and hearing along with a capacity to drift, hover and wait on the wind by almost stealing the breeze, would be of no value if the targets, short-tailed field voles in the case of the barn owl, were aware of the predator's presence.

Owls hunt in low light levels at dusk and dawn, so the chances of them being seen by their targets is much reduced. However, there is still the problem of intrusive noise emanating from the wings because mice, particularly, can hear really well.

So barn owls, having evolved over thousands of years, now have flight feathers that deaden very efficiently any sound they might otherwise make. The leading fore-edge and the outer part of the trailing edge of these feathers are equipped with rigid barbs while the upper surfaces are downy or 'super-soft', thus 'soaking up the sound'.

Silent flight is important to owls, enabling their sense of hearing, their 'ear slits' are asymmetrically placed on the facial discs, to function unhindered by backgound noise.

In Bristol, in the early '50s, starlings and house sparrows were everywhere.

Here, in North Devon, the starlings are now steadily disappearing, reflecting 50% drop in their num over the past 25 years.

Yet, we still have a good winter roost under the Old Bridge crossing the River Torridge!

At home, we still have a good flock of sparrows and five species of tits, too. The Marsh tits are favourites, along with the great-spotted woodpeckers.

© John Threlfall, 2007
www.johnthrelfall.co.uk

After my first truly unforgettable and my many subsequent visits to the Severn Wildfowl Trust during 1950 and 1951, I would write to Peter Scott, telling him of my experiences.

One of the highlights of those first occasions was to join fifteen or so visitors late in the afternoon in the Big Pen. Here we were introduced to a large crowd of irrepressible ducks, geese and swans, by a person who would be dressed casually in fur-lined naval jacket, white polo-necked sweater and carrying a pair of Ross 10 x 60 binoculars. Standing well out in the pool, the forty year old Peter Scott would hand feed his birds. He would speak in an informal and friendly manner about the various individuals that scurried and dived in front of him as they searched for the grains of wheat. He would explain his aims for the Trust and its collection. Scott was often accompanied by friends and fellow naturalists; I now know that the eminent sound-recordist Ludwig Koch was one; another was Konrad Lorenz, animal behaviourist and the author of King Solomon's Ring, which threw new light on animal behaviour and was years ahead of its time. In his collection in the Bavarian Alps, Lorenz recorded the imprinting of greylag goslings on their parents.

I told Peter Scott of the joy of my first redshanks and sent him the photograph of the nest with its four eggs, which I had discovered at Portbury Wharf. The Bristol Waterworks Company was creating Chew Valley Lake and as the reservoir's waters deepened, there were increasing numbers and varieties of wildfowl. A telescope now backed up my field glasses. Close-up views of wigeon, teal, pintail,

My Whoopers, descendants of wild birds, were a prolific pair
Whooper Swan, *Cygnus cygnus*.
© John and Tracy Langley, Chester. www.ourwildlifephotography.co.uk

gadwall and great crested grebe, both the latter species were soon breeding widely, were now taken for granted. Diving species, pochard and tufted, became ever-present and in winter-time we were regularly watching wildfowl at which I had either only previously gazed at in my reference books or had spotted as individuals in the growing Slimbridge collection. Suddenly smew, goldeneye, scaup, red breasted merganser and goosander were, literally, at the other end of the powerful 'scope.

In another letter a few years later, I suggested that the Trust might consider a junior membership club. In due course, in 1957, the 'Goslings' were formed and Nicola Scott, Peter Scott's eldest daughter was its first member; I was delighted to become the club's first public junior member.

There were to be three levels of membership decided by increasingly difficult identification tests; you could become a greylag, pinkfoot or a whitefront. For my final examination I was introduced, formally for the first time to Peter Scott in the Orchard Pen by Diana Johnstone, wife of the curator Tommy Johnstone. Diana was responsible for the remarkable growth in the gift shop sales, providing the Trust not only with much needed extra revenue, but also for putting the Trust's name and its reputation in front of a much larger and potential visiting public.

I scraped through my test, just! Forty-five out of fifty. Peter Scott then paused and picking up some feathers, asked me to identify the species from which they had been moulted. I was flummoxed.

"When you are able to identify individual feathers as well as the birds, then you will truly know your wildfowl." His remark was not intended to chide, but was made with warmth and a friendly smile of which I was to become very fond for the next thirty-five years.

On a summer's day in the 80s I was filming with the BBC NHU at Slimbridge with my pair of tame barn owls. On the same day, Peter Scott was working with ITV's Anglia 'Survival' production team. Our paths did not cross and there was no need for them to do so. By early evening, I had completed my brief. I was returning both birds to their blocks in the vehicle before going home when Peter Scott appeared. He apologised for not coming to see me sooner but had been told about 'the beautiful owls'.

"If you've a moment I'd love to see them," he began. I rolled back the hessian sacking. Both birds stared at him and rotated their heads through 180 degrees, out of curiosity and affection.

Scott, as was his custom dropped his glasses off the bridge of his nose, and peered intently and quietly at them.

"Tell me," he started, "the black flecks on the breast of the one bird; and also that very dark ochre edging to the tips of the feathers on the facial disc mean what?" he added, pointing unobtrusively.

"That's the female," I answered, explaining that the male has much paler breast feathers, almost pure white, with no spots and that, in fact, when alongside one another you can see that the male is smaller. Scott closely observed both birds, captivated by their delicate beauty, a magic almost beyond words which is still readily appreciated by audiences today at my 'Face to Face' presentations.

"Have you finished with the BBC for today?", he asked.

"Other than saying my goodbyes to the director and crew, yes."

"Would you like a drink, a whiskey or a gin and tonic perhaps? Come over to the studio, and bring the owls why don't you. I could sketch the differences."

That spontaneous invitation summarised Peter Scott, the naturalist. He was always seeking and was truly fascinated by new knowledge. He also possessed a humility so rarely apparent in the present day 'media' naturalists; he would listen and take on board the knowledge of a self-taught enthusiastic amateur for whom natural history was, and still is, a lifetime's interest. Today, so many of the 'experts' have previously been the 'expert' in another field before switching, courtesy of a good agent, to extend their media longevity.

I recall Scott's encouragement to learn my wildfowl feathers. But sharing the detailed variations in the feathers of the barn owls with him that summer's evening at Slimbridge meant that the wheel had turned full circle and, very briefly, our roles had been reversed. He was a lovely man, so friendly, always giving me the opportunity to talk personally; I still miss him many years after his passing.

*"When the moon is clear ... and the wild geese come in ... and the tide whispers up ... then I think that I understand ... It's life to a man who can understand ... it shall be life for me ... then when the geese come in ... **through me all men shall understand.**"*
Extract from 'A Picture of Geese'
Lt Comdr Sir Peter Scott CBE DSC 1909-1989

Peter Scott addressing guests at the opening of the Wildlife Park and British Nature Centre at Westbury-on-Trym, Bristol, in early June 1967.
photo: Jim Hale, 1967, courtesy Mia Hale

Meanwhile, in the very early months of the Gosling Club, I received an invitation to appear in a BBC Children's Television 'live' Outside Broadcast to be transmitted from Scott's studio window overlooking the Rushy Pen. The programme would widely promote the launch of the 'Goslings' and would encourage young viewers nationwide to become junior members of the Trust.

With permission from school, I arrived well in time for the afternoon's rehearsals. The live transmission would be at teatime. I was to accompany Peter Scott around the main pond, step into the studio and sit down to identify, from monitor sets, different wildfowl selected by the cameramen. However, as I was readily recognising the various individuals, Peter Scott thought the youngsters at home would suspect that the pictures were pre-planned. He suggested to the director that I should make a deliberate mistake; he could then break the rather too simple dialogue of "what's this one?" followed by the inevitable correct answer from me allowing him to insert a descriptive identification in his own inimitable style.

I would muddle the red-crested pochard, *Netta rufina* with the rosybill, *Netta peposaca*. The cameramen were primed to pick up these two species simultaneously. All the birds on the pond had been left unfed until just before the broadcast, so that they would 'throng' close-by. The calculated 'gaffe' went to plan, allowing Scott to remind me and the viewers that one way to avoid the mistake was to "remember that the orange-red crest of the male red-crested pochard resembled a badger-hair shaving brush."

Over thirty years later, and as I have recorded elsewhere, I filmed with Gerald Durrell and my hand-tame trio of badgers on location. I recall how I was introduced by the director to the several individuals with whom I would be working. With these completed, he turned and looking directly at me, said, "And you still don't recognize me, do you?"

"I have absolutely no idea," I responded, somewhat taken out of my stride, "I do apologise."

He continued looking me straight in the eye and smiling, continued, "You and I last met when I directed that outside television broadcast from Peter Scott's studio window You had to make that planned mistake with those two ducks, d'ye remember?"

"Yes, the red-crested pochard and the rosybill"

"You must have been about fifteen at the time. Well I'm Peter Bale and it's good to see you again. Small world, isn't it?"

The sudden arrival of those redshanks on the wet mud of an ebbing tide on a Saturday afternoon over fifty years ago proved to be a turning point in my young life.

I can still recognise the excitement, the thrill that occurs as soon as I first spot a gang of small brownish-grey waders, knowing that they continue to be difficult to recognise. I experience the inevitable frustration as they constantly move on chasing the water's edge, leaving a blur of white bars, white rumps, trailing legs and piping calls all of which still muddle me, leaving me in confusion all these years later. Yes, I'm alright on curlew, lapwing, oyster catcher and nowadays golden plover, bar-tailed godwit, ringed plover and, of course, redshank, but all those other little browny-grey chaps on spring and autumn passage, well ...

However, whenever I see my favourite birds, wildfowl and waders, I am sure to be in my special places. They are the wide and flat marshes, lying close to snaking tidal creeks and the winding channels of the saltings. Saltings that melt into mudflats and they, in turn, into flat and shining estuaries.

The author, with Jack Griffith, at Fremington Quay overlooking the Taw Estuary, and the very place where he saw his first redshank in the 'Land of the Two Rivers'
© and courtesy of Olivia Chaffe, 2007

Never in my wildest dreams would I have thought that fifty-five years later, another young boy, Jack Griffith, would enjoy a experience, similar to mine on the River Avon near Bristol, but this time in North Devon. Jack saw his redshank at the mouth of the beautiful estuary of the River Taw, close to our home in the Land of the Two Rivers. Here is his written account of that event.

On a rainy, blustery day in October, I was on holiday with my family in Devon, and we were cycling from Braunton to Barnstaple on the Tarka Trail.

Braunton is the most beautiful place in the world for me. The huge open beach has silky sand, and the wind blows beautiful patterns on it. The old railway track wraps around the estuary from there up to Barnstaple.

The tide was out, so we had stopped to look at the birds out on the mud, shovelling and poking in the mud to find food. We heard a high-pitched peeping, and a flock of oyster catchers flew by. This was followed by a long bubbling call from a curlew.

The rain stopped, the wind died down, and then we noticed, among the oyster catchers, a slender bird slowly picking its way through the mud. It was a beautiful redshank with orange legs and speckled feathers. We watched it for a minute or two and then it flew up and circled over our heads twice before heading off across the estuary in the direction of Appledore. It was a wonderful rare sight for me and I will never forget it.

Redshank, *Tringa totanus*, by Jack Griffith, aged 11. The winner of the 8-12 yr old age group in the RSPB annual 'Wild Art' Competition; exhibited at the Mall Galleries, London, Sept '05, alongside The Society of Wildlife Artists Annual Exhibition.

Jack Griffith

Jack Griffith, aged 11

* Stop Press: Red-legged Partridge, *Alectoris rufa*, also by Jack Griffith, the runner-up in the 13-18 yr age group, 2007.

Thank you, Jack, for contributing to *Face to Face with Nature*; I gather your beautiful artwork has been further recognised elsewhere*. I hope you will continue to pursue your interest in and undoubted talent for wild nature in the wild places where it lives.

Redshanks have been part and parcel of my life for a long time now; I still see them most days, frequently within yards of our home. Unobtrusive and delicate, their presence serves as a constant reminder of how we continue to hijack the environment. Their wetland homes are increasingly threatened; their fragility and wild ways, which are tied so closely to the rhythm of the tides, tell me they are part of a much greater scheme of things, something so magical which too few people find the time to appreciate. We have destroyed and continue to threaten the places where they live; the sad thing is that we know we are doing it; my despair is that we have the resources to do something about it, to reverse the process, even to stop it altogether. But, we lack the will; it's not that we don't care, we just don't care enough.

We need so many more youngsters like Jack Griffith.

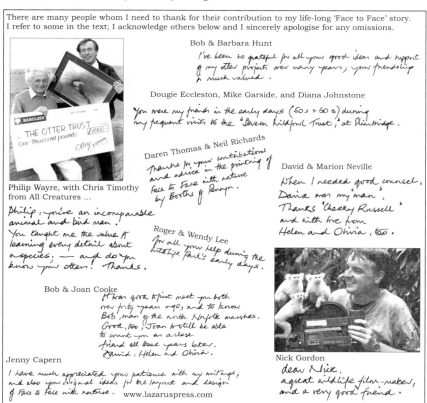

There are many people whom I need to thank for their contribution to my life-long 'Face to Face' story. I refer to some in the text; I acknowledge others below and I sincerely apologise for any omissions.

Bob & Barbara Hunt

I've been so grateful for all your good ideas and support of my otter projects over many years; your friendship is much valued.

Dougie Eccleston, Mike Garside, and Diana Johnstone

You were my friends in the early days (50 s & 60 s) during my frequent visits to the "Severn Wildfowl Trust", at Slimbridge.

Daren Thomas & Neil Richards

Thanks for your contributions and advice in the printing of Face to Face with nature by Booths of Penryn.

David & Marion Neville

When I needed good council, David was my 'man'. Thanks 'Cheeky Russell' and with love from Helen and Olivia, too.

Philip Wayre, with Chris Timothy from All Creatures ...

Philip, you're an incomparable animal and bird man. You taught me the value of learning every detail about a species; — and do you know your otters! Thanks.

Roger & Wendy Lee

For all your help during the wildlife park's early days.

Bob & Joan Cooke

It was good to first meet you both over forty years ago, and to know Bob, man of the north Norfolk marshes. Good, too, Joan to still be able to count you an a close friend all these years later. David, Helen and Olivia.

Jenny Capern

I have much appreciated your patience with my writings, and also your original ideas for the layout and design of Face to Face with nature. www.lazaruspress.com

Nick Gordon

dear Nick, a great wildlife film-maker, and a very good friend.

136

"Will you come and talk to our Rotary Club about your Wildlife Park? I'm sure we'd all be fascinated."

I was sitting in the first XV changing room of Clifton Rugby Club. The question had come from a previous captain, Mike 'Bones' Moss, after a hard-fought victory over arch-rivals, Lydney. I was alongside my fellow members of the 'back row', Bob Osborn and Grant Watson.

"You go and tell them, Daktari," Grant answered for me. "Tell them about those deer you've got roaming in the woods, they'll love it." Grant had lumbered me with that nickname. I wore contact lenses and, previously, he had told everyone in earshot at the club's bar that I reminded him of the cross-eyed lion of that name which was, then, a character on our television screens.

The venue was The Miners' Arms in Bedminster, close to Ashton Gate, the home of Bristol City Football Club. It was my first public presentation and I'm afraid I read the whole of my speech. Nevertheless, the audience were enthusiastic, with many wishing me well and saying that they were looking forward to visiting with their families after the planned opening in June 1967, by Peter Scott. Many then returned to work, but one question took me by surprise.

"Do you want a golden eagle for your Park?"

"You mean a golden eagle? You're not joking?"

"No, I'm not. Seriously, I know where there is one. I've seen it; it was tied to a large block. It's at Weston Park, that's near Birmingham. Fantastic looking bird. Why don't you give them a ring? You never know, they might just part with it."

I was very excited returning to the Park with my first golden eagle, which was in fact, a large adult female. It was December time and past midnight. I had spent some time getting to know and handle the bird which had been trained to fly to the glove. She came complete with a block to which she was now tethered and on which she would eventually be displayed to my visitors. Surrounded for her own safety by straw bales on three sides, my access to her was via the side loading door immediately behind the driver's door.

I left the M5 motorway and was now only ten minutes driving time from the Park. As I came over the railway bridge on the dual carriageway link road, I was suddenly approaching a police road block which had been cleverly positioned; it was invisible until drivers were on the apex of the bridge. I slowed to a halt between the lines of cones, and opened the driver's window as an officer approached.

"Good evening, sir, I'd be obliged if you'd answer a few questions."

I thought I would have some fun; after all, there was nothing that suspicious or illegal in driving a van into Bristol late at night.

"Could you tell me the registration number of your vehicle?"

"I have no idea," I replied bluntly.

The young policeman appeared to be taken aback.

"Then, could you show me your driving license, please?"

"I'm sorry, I'm not carrying any documents with me," I answered.

"Would you tell me what you are carrying?"

"A golden eagle," I stated abruptly, whilst still trying to maintain a disinterested and unconcerned look on my face.

Although hand-tame, my golden eagle could suddenly look very aggressive.
© and courtesy Richard Gibson, The Zoological Society of London

"Really sir!" said the policeman raising his eyebrows. He realised he was getting nowhere fast. But, before he could continue another officer, a rather portly sergeant approached. He pulled himself together, rose on both soles of his feet, we all have this image of 'Mr Plod', don't we, and no, he did not say 'warm night, warm night', but rather ...

"Any problems, Jones?"

"Well, Sarge," Jones replied, clearly ruffled, "this gentlemen says he has no idea of his vehicle's registration number, no documents, no identity and has just told me he's carrying a golden eagle."

Then the sergeant leaned forward and, simultaneously, opened the driver's door. He beckoned with the other hand. "Shall we get out, sir?" I slipped out. "Thank you, sir."

Straightaway, he gesticulated again, this time pointing to the side loading door and said in an irritated tone, "shall we open this door, too, sir?"

Without saying a word, I slid the door back and there was this huge bird. Eagles can look frightening at four feet, especially when lit by flashing blue lights.

The sergeant never spoke to me, but turning to the young officer, said, "Carry on Jones," and walked away. It was at that moment I caught sight of several other officers falling about laughing at both the sergeant's, and Jones', undoubted embarrassment.

"Carry on Jones..."

"He doesn't know 'is registration number - he's got no Driving Licence and he's just told me he's carrying a **GOLDEN EAGLE** Sarge!"

Madagascar split from mainland Africa 100 million years ago, resulting in the evolution of a unique fauna and flora. The red-bellied lemur, *Eulemur rubriventer*, is a primate unique to the island with fossil remains dating back 50 million years. Now, all the lemurs are threatened by rainforest destruction, with most facing extinction. Madagascar is one of the world's fifteen poorest countries, with the lowest level of health spending in Africa at $15 per head ... yet ... just 4% of the wealth of the world's 225 richest families would provide the basic health care, education and nutrition for the whole world!

I met the Frontier UK team at London Heathrow for the Diving and Marine Conservation expedition; after collecting our equipment, we flew British Midland Airways to Paris' Charles de Gaulle airport before transferring to an Air Madagascar flight, 6000 miles non-stop to the capital, Antanarivo.

From there, it was another internal flight north followed by a boat trip and finally a long walk to Manta Camp. Manta would be my home for the next few weeks and we were given just a few days to settle in. We soon started to split the jobs; taking it in turns to carry out the camp duties; then we commenced surveying the coastal waters and bays.

My first and lasting memorable experience will always be so many species of fish and forms of corals of such amazing colours. Much of the time I didn't know where to look first. Of course, I was diving for the first time, too. I went on to lead a team dive and obtained my PADI certificate by diving to a depth of 70ft; (open water and advanced open water). We often saw rare turtles along with Parrot fish, Lion fish and Barracuda.

One thing I will never forget was seeing a giant Manta Ray. The gracefulness of such a large fish was unbelievable and most definitely the highlight of the Madagascan experience; it was awesome! On one occasion when I was swimming backstroke, a large fish swam into me ... and the night dive was wicked.

I learnt so much, saw incredible sights and made some great friends. Then I waved them goodbye before travelling by boat across the bay from Manta camp to a small village, Antisikala. Here, I taught the children English every day for four weeks, and learnt a little Malagasy myself!

The difference in the way of life between us and the native islanders is shocking. Madagascans live in small huts, slightly raised off the ground and in small communities. They grow, pound and sort rice and catch fish. The children help with all the work and have few options to go to school in the nearest town. I now know you cannot fully understand the situation in Madagascar until you have experienced it for yourself.

After all my experiences so far, I hope to carry out conservation work and, most importantly I want to further people's knowledge of the natural world. I want to make a difference, or, at least, start making a difference in the world of conservation.

This is my brief record of the last 3½ months; I am writing it whilst looking down on the Sahara Desert on the 12th of July 2006 as I head home, via Paris to London. We were 24 hours late leaving because there was no fuel at the International Airport at Antanarivo!

Olivia Chaffe

Manta Ray, *Manta birostris*

sources: Earth from the Air;
a photographic portrait of our planet.
Yann Arhus-Bertrand, 2006.

It was a sunlit autumn evening in mid-October and at around half-past five I was counting the day's takings in the small admission gatehut of my Wildlife Park. The scattering of afternoon visitors had drifted away; the collection's great variety of native British animals and birds had been fed and everything was now still in the valley.

The many mature trees, the elms, oaks and willows, were shedding their leaves and recent heavy squally showers had accelerated the fall. The rain also meant that the River Trym, which flowed through the grounds from the adjacent Badocks Woods, had a good volume of flowing water again following the relative trickle of late summer. The memories of this valley have lingered in my mind over a lifetime. Even in the late 1960s, it frustrated me knowing that its beauty was so unappreciated by the half million residents of my home City of Bristol. Fifty years, later with a thriving community junior school just a couple of hundred yards away, its charm and value as a natural teaching resource is still rarely enjoyed, or shared, even by local residents.

In the few years since taking over the long abandoned eleven acres, many unexpected wild animals and birds, other than the usual seasonal migrants, had become residents. I had actively encouraged many after their first and unanticipated appearances.

Early mornings and late afternoons became the most favoured times to observe the kingfishers. We had constructed a dam across the Trym halfway along the river paddock. The wall of the dam, with its waterfall, was just downstream below a rank of well-grown willow trees, whose thick lower boughs reached out over the now deep stretch of water immediately behind the construction.

Shoals of sticklebacks and minnows had quickly become established. These were the plentiful food source to which the kingfishers regularly returned, with the dense foliage providing the ideal cover from which to launch their plunging and lightning strikes.

I wasted so much time waiting for their periodic appearances; I watched them, using my field glasses, from the sanctuary of the café building just down river. I had seen kingfishers before and had always admired, albeit briefly, their stunning plumage. But it was in the Park that for the first time, I appreciated the marginal difference between the sexes. The lower mandible of the female is red. Some years later, when explaining the variation to a visitor, who had been also lucky enough to spot an azure blue dart arriving to take up its favourite feeding perch, she had commented, "so the female bird is just like us; she wears lipstick, too!"

In 2007, I can still watch kingfishers everyday if I so wish, especially at Beam Weir on the Torridge, halcyon hunters alongside their other river neighbours, dippers, grey wagtails and, of course, otters.

It was in the same river enclosure that I had established a pair of Whooper Swans. I had collected them from Whipsnade Zoo along with a small flock of tufted duck. After only one winter in which to settle, they nested successfully. One evening that summer, having worked late, I treated myself to a steak supper in the 'Hole in the Wall' restaurant, a 'Berni' steak house in Queen's Square, Bristol. From there I would travel on to my home in Nempnett Thrubwell, a small hamlet made up of dairy farms and cottages overlooking Blagdon Lake and the Mendip Hills in north Somerset. As I crossed College Green, I met Peter Scott leaving the venue. He was accompanied by Mike Garside, one of his personal secretaries. During our conversation, I mentioned the Whoopers' success.

"I know about the history and parentage of those birds," Scott confided. "They're direct descendants of a wild-caught pair which eventually found their way into the private collection of a Dutchman by the name of van Schuyl. That was back in the early '30s."

I gained the distinct impression that Scott had desires on my individuals and thus their breeding strain for the Slimbridge collection. They were a prolific pair, strongly defining their territory and becoming very robust and protective parents. They were a constant delight for visitors. I first spotted them on a chance visit to Whipsnade, whilst looking for individual deer to add to my family groups. It was a matter of being in the right place at the right time!

Four pairs of pinioned mallard from my own collection were among the very first residents when I created my Wildlife Park. The birds bred well, coping with the interference from the other livestock and particularly, the many hundreds of visitors who would descend on the eleven acres at weekends and on traditional bank holidays during spring and summer time. Mallards breed early, with their first broods always hatched by Eastertime. But it was a devil's own job rescuing youngsters from all manner of desperate and perilous situations. Individuals, or whole broods, would first be heard cheeping plaintively, whilst usually remaining unseen, before being eventually and, inevitably, first discovered by visitors.

On one occasion, a few had somehow gained access into one of the hawk aviaries, where they were definitely living on borrowed time! We successfully collected some others that were still surviving in the grey seal pool; the large mammals were bemused by the ducklings who bobbed around like corks amongst them; it was amazing to see the seals nudging them with their long Roman noses; they could have just as easily swallowed them whole! Another time, a crowd had again quickly gathered, visitors always seemed to appear from nowhere when they were least wanted; we were attempting to retrieve ducklings from the depths of the World Wildlife Fund's wishing well in a bucket. The word 'pantomime' springs to mind.

Nevertheless, despite all the potential setbacks and along with some full-winged gifts and the occasional wild birds that latched on to the regular twice-daily feeds, a flock of nearly thirty birds had become resident on the river. Early this autumn evening they had again set out on their regular sortie, which saw them twisting and turning in rapid flight towards the village of nearby Westbury-on-Trym, the ducks calling loudly as they were chased and tracked by their chosen mates. I watched them circle the church, they regularly used the tower as their distant marker, before turning back towards the Trym valley within the Park. They never strayed too far; safety for them was their favourite stretch of the river. Their noisy splashdown as they 'fell' vertically, breaking hard, was a constant joy to watch. Immediately, upon their return there would be an excited interchange of gossip with another half dozen disabled waifs and strays bequeathed by friends of the Park. These birds, through no fault of their own, were sadly never able to join their full-winged friends, but still had their safe semi-freedom on the river.

On one particular occasion when I was about to leave the Park, luck favoured me. I spotted, for the first time, a wild heron standing close to the water's edge along the river pen. Its inherent nervousness had clearly been somewhat overcome by his or her misunderstanding of why all the local inhabitants, the ducks and moorhens, the swans and even the pair of hand-reared Chinese water deer which were a gift from the Showering Estates at Shepton Mallet, were so unfazed by the strange goings-on so alien to feral creatures. I returned quickly to the stable yard and in the food preparation room, scavenged through a waste bin to retrieve several half-eaten remains of dead day-old chicks. They would have been collected earlier that day from the hawk and owl aviaries. I returned towards the river pen and, by creeping ever closer from behind a clump of dogwood bushes, which formed one boundary and gave good cover, I lobbed the scraps in the direction of my wild visitor. I then left. As I locked the main gates the heron had still not been

By four o'clock most afternoons, the herons would have taken up their favourite vantage points.
© Peter Partington, 2007.
www.peterpartington.fsnet.co.uk

142

frightened. He or she was still montionless, apparently undisturbed, although probably somewhat bewildered staring at a free evening meal only a short distance away.

I reminded my staff to make sure some scraps of fish and chicks were regularly left close to the river's edge at the end of every day. At that time, there were already up to half a dozen Atlantic grey and common seals so there would be ample leftovers for this first heron as well as any future companions. Inevitably other scavengers, crows and magpies, would be encouraged; nevertheless my plan worked. On another evening, a few weeks later and not long after the mallards' return, three herons who had been spotted standing patiently, statuesque in the surrounding tall trees, flapped down to feed. Their coarse 'krank' like calls were in stark contrast to the tranquility of the valley.

These wild herons, sometimes there were up to five individuals, would always stay throughout the early winter months. By four o'clock most afternoons, having beat in slowly on great convex arches of wings with long legs stretched our behind short square tails, they would have taken up their favourite vantage points. Then they would wait, their long necks hunched back into their shoulders, a couple on the river bank, others perhaps long-legged on fence posts; but,

A male kingfisher, *Alcedo atthis*; the lower mandible of the female is coloured red; "so the female bird is just like us, she wears lipstick too!" a visitor at the Wildlife Park remarked nearly forty years ago
© John and Tracy Langley, Chester
www.ourwildlifephotography.co.uk

being early nesters, they had departed by early February every year. I never did discover the local heronry which they favoured. I guess it was much further away than I imagined; neither did the number of birds increase, nor were there any signs that they would stay to nest for I never spotted courtship behaviour. The trees would have been entirely suitable but, of course, I was never sure that my visitors were always the same individuals. I never saw any juveniles, young birds of the year; was it always non-breeding adults, with their yellow heads and black and silver lace-like feathers around haggard necks, which lived on the fringes of family groups, that were our visitors? Maybe it was, "it's your turn for a freebie tonight, courtesy of the Wildlife Park." Was that part of the heron's vocabulary? Eventually, I reckoned that the heronry was ancestral and probably very large and close to the River Severn several miles to the west.

So, this October evening was no different. I had quickly learned to recognise the different tones of the herons conversations, whenever one indiviual argued with another over the choice of a particular leftover. Then, I would worry whether my member of staff had remembered to scatter the carcases over a wide enough area, so that the most dominant bird did not devour the lion's share of the food. Herons do have voracious appetites.

At that moment, my thoughts were disturbed by a female voice. "I'm so sorry to bother you at this late hour, and I realise you're about to close, but do you think, or rather, would it be possible to purchase some day-old chicks? Dead ones, of course. Maybe a dozen or so perhaps?"

Initially, I was rather taken aback. One or two people had previously requested a dead chick for feeding to a pet snake. Others had asked if I would sell in bulk, for more people were keeping hawks and owls as a hobby; but this enquiry was clearly of a different nature. The lady was well dressed and didn't appear to be in any way an individual who kept the kind of livestock at home which would regularly eat day-old chicks. She could clearly see that I had been caught unawares, so continued.

"I will willingly pay you for them. Would a pound cover the cost?"

"I'll go and fetch some," I spluttered. "Did you say a dozen?"

"Please, if you can spare them."

I accepted the money on my return, but finally my curiosity got the better of me.

"Excuse me asking but ..." Before I could continue the visitor interrupted me.

"I thought you might ask. You see, my husband is a senior executive working on the construction programme for the Concorde airliners at Filton. You will probably know that everything is being done in collaboration with the French factory in Toulouse. Well, some of my husband's French counterparts are coming to supper during their visit to see the progress on the two prototypes at Filton. I have to entertain them, you see. I am going to use the chicks as a starter for the meal which I am preparing."

"As the starter?" I enquired, incredulously.

"Yes, I will skin them and season well, before pan frying them in garlic and butter!'

"Really," was the extent of my reply.

I handed over the chicks; the starter must have been a success for my visitor returned on at least a couple of other occasions. However, I have never got my head around 'le petit poussin a la beurre' as a starter!

Afterword

"Every one of us can still make a difference ... yes, we really can!"

Polar Bear: *Ursus maritimus*
© John Threlfall
www.johnthrelfall.co.uk

The average thickness of the Arctic Ice Field has dropped from
3.12m in the 1960s to below 1.8m in the year 2006; the Arctic perennial
sea ice, which survives the summer melt season and remains year-round,
shrank by 14 % in just twelve months between 2004 and 2005, an area of
720,000 sq km, almost the size of Turkey ...

Satellite navigation is telling us that the Arctic sea ice has retreated over past decades from
between 5 to 15 % extending, therefore, the ice-free summers by up to three weeks. Every week
cuts the amount of fat a polar bear will have accumulated by the outset of winter by 10 to 20 kg.
The implications are colossal. By 2050, within three polar bear generations, numbers are expected to fall. It could mean the extinction, in the lifetime of children alive today, of the polar bear,
which needs the floating banks of ice to reach its prey, seals. Remember, too, that ice is part of
the biology of every creature that lives in this frozen vastness.

sources: Claire Parkinson, NASA and The Scott Polar Research Institute, Cambridge University 2006

It is impressive watching these birds against the huge ice cliffs

Black Browed Albatross / S + L & Ca Pigeon

head study
note bill shape
& colour - black eye brow

reduced nostril (tube) this is also a gland for removing salt

reddish on breeding adult

huge long w

Brown/black above

Bowed huge wings

Blackish tail

White body

Cape pigeons a small petrel black & wh in plumage

White quills to outer primaries

Wings wider than a story
The last albatross speeds silently across the oc
Wings moving like a song
Like the last star in the sky
Albatross, in all her glory
And the story might be over
Speeds along
And the song might say Goodbye

Extract from 'The Albatross' © Ian McMillan, Yorkshire poet, broadcaster and comedian
by kind permission of the RSPB Bird Life magazine (May/June 2006)
Black-browed albatross, *Diomedea melanophris*, off South Georgia, west of the South Sandwich Islands, 1000
miles north of the Antarctic Circle and the maximum amount of the sea ice stretching from the Weddell Sea.
© Steve Cale, 2006. www.steve-cale-artist.co.uk

So, it is the last days of August 2007 and I am closing the *Face to Face with Nature* story. I write most frequently at a place where I stop twice daily and at varying times. I take time to observe the same short stretch of the river Torridge which is fully tidal at this point. Halspill Creek is five miles upstream from where the river's muddy waters, flowing sluggishly for most of the year except when in freshwater spate after winter rains, first meet the Atlantic currents in sight of Lundy. Here, the river's edges are flanked either by steep densely-wooded banks or by low-lying water meadows, whose river-bank boundaries are breached by the higher spring and autumn tides.

At first glance, little has changed hereabouts during the eight years since we have been living in the Land of the Two Rivers. In the short distance from here to our cottage home only one barn renovation has been completed. However, within the main village of Weare Giffard, several new homes have been constructed and that significant expansion has been happening to a similar degree in other communities throughout rural Devon. Another four hundred thousand homes to be built in the county over the next decade was the figure being floated by the Rural Development Agency in mid-June. Clearly much of this figure

As early as April, woodlands all over the British Isles can be red-violet or pink purple with the earliest flowering of our orchids. They can grow in abundance, whilst another year there may be only a few. The plant very often dies after flowering and its development from seed to plant can take several years and this is evident when the seed has set badly.

Few of us will be lucky enough to travel to Antarctica and to see amongst the continent's teeming wildlife, black-browed albatrosses. Many more of us, however, will appreciate the orchids of our countryside ... but remember both are very much part of the wild nature of planet earth and both, in their own way, are equally stunning and beautiful.

Early purple Orchid, *Orchis mascula*, and Marsh Helleborine, *Epipactis palustris*
© and courtesy Sue Frost, Weare Giffard, North Devon, 2007

would include the urban expansion around Plymouth and Exeter and the dominant 'market' towns; there are also plans for two 'new' towns, in the Sherford valley to the east of Plymouth, (details for 5,500 homes were adopted 07/08 '07), and also in the South Hams. Indeed these developments are being mirrored throughout most rural counties.

At this moment in the early evening and with a three-quarter tide running strongly in the estuary, the locally-born young swallows and house martins are on the wing all around me. They are this summer's successes, and have been gathering with greater frequency in a loose family group, especially towards the end of every day. They are familiarising themselves with their immediate surroundings. This is an important process so that they can return after the coming autumn and winter away, to the very same barns and outbuildings which were the sites of their original nurseries. There are nowhere near as many youngsters amongst the flock as in previous years; indeed, fewer adult pairs returned in the spring. Nevertheless, a couple of late broods may yet boost numbers. The juveniles of both species are easily recognisable from the adults, appearing dumpy with no long tail streamers.

As the swallows and martins, whose very presence during the summer months reflects for me the magic of an English summer, are preparing for their departure, the shelducks are only just beginning to drift back from their summer moulting grounds in any numbers. Inevitably, the river has been quieter without their noisy conversations. You can always hear their distinctive small talk before catching a glimpse of them; with typical arching of necks and heads when a point is being stressed to a mate or neighbours, they dabble in wet flashes amongst the long vegetation. Half a dozen clearly defined pairs were feeding contentedly in separate places during April which, however, was unseasonally warm. Sadly though, in June, there was a dearth of youngsters scampering across the wet mud; I saw no ducklings, whereas in previous summers, a crèche twenty to thirty strong with accompanying mothers and aunties, is what I have come to expect. As well as being cold and wet, we had our June weather in April, an unexpected and quickly resident pair of greater black-backed gulls, with their bullying and marauding tactics, must have also greatly lessened the chances of any ducklings that were surviving the inclement weather.

Whilst waiting, watching and writing in my vehicle during summer days, the still common species of butterfly are always close at hand. There's something intriguing yet frustrating about them as I watch their antics and I have a similar feeling as the bats exit their roosts at dusk on warm summer evenings. Both are energetic but the butterflies show off vivid yet delicate colours. My favourites, because I see fewer of them, are the peacocks. However, speckled woods are plentiful, with individuals seemingly endlessly chasing one another. Then, just as quickly, they suddenly disappear without trace amongst the cow parsley and foxgloves in the overgrown hedgerows.

There are numerous small tortoiseshells, red admirals, meadow browns and gatekeepers too, each species suddenly more noticeable at different times during summer. Habitat loss and the intensification of agriculture are reasons for their decline; however, numbers stay good here. Maybe there is only piecemeal clearance of an area from time to time and on a small scale, which allows the butterflies to follow the changes. They suffer when there is large scale destruction. I use the field glasses at close range, but haven't read enough about butterfly behaviour to understand, for example, their zig-zagging and, for me, apparently carefree flights.

I witnessed a typical early spring migration this year. It was good to see whimbrel staying fleetingly in early May before moving north to their summer nesting grounds in Shetland, Orkney and Iceland. Over twenty years ago Helen and I would watch for them as they stopped briefly in other favourite meadows, those near Burtle on the Somerset Levels. By late July, early August, the first of the non-breeding waders were already on their return passage and as in previous years, I caught brief glimpses of greenshanks, common and green sandpipers, the latter's white rumps clearly unmistakable; nevertheless, the first individuals of the large flock of blackheaded gulls, still sporting the dark chocolate heads of their breeding plumage, were already back. Inevitably, they will now stay well into next spring on the wet mud and always at the edge of the tide. Their constant strident calls confirm that estuary life is returning to its normal routines, after the very short summer break.

During any brief stay I always spot at least one individual from either of the local buzzard or raven families. This time I heard the emphatic 'kronk' call of the latter; it was an adult returning to its favourite roosting haunt in nearby Beam Quarry. At this time of year each bird is only gently going through the motions of reinforcing their territory, but during the short winter days after Christmas, I sometimes wonder whether they can afford to spend so much time quarrelling.

The jackdaws and pied wagtails are friendly and inquisitive; tonight, they seem determined to seek my company. The jackdaws have bred in the chimneys and outbuildings of the farm nearby; the wagtails have brought up two broods. There's always plenty of insect life around the food troughs and amongst the piles of dung. They have clearly identified the live food amongst the droppings from the flock of Suffolk rams which will serve the farmer's seven hundred or so mule x breeding ewes.

Of greater significance and a huge disappointment has been the loss of the yellow hammers from the higher pastures close to our home. They have been conspicuous residents since we moved from west Cornwall, where they were also with us all year round. I miss seeing these canary-yellow buntings; they would obligingly sit tight on the telephone wires; on many an occasion, a buzzard and a raven would be on adjoining telegraph poles with the tiny buntings on the wires between.

Not around this year, too, and always visible before choosing their nest site at the foot of the densest hedgerow, have been the summer-visiting whitethroats. We may have missed them on their arrival and the June weather could have been responsible for their demise, as with the shelducks. However, climate change will surely be affecting their winter territories in Africa but, as yet, we still know few details.

There has been considerable diversification in local farming practices, sometimes after needless events, following the tragic Foot and Mouth disaster in 2001. So it is promising that we can still see and hear our skylarks all year round. Helen and I spot red-legged partridges, pheasants and barn owls, too, along with several hares which gently amble before us, as we walk our dogs along the top lane.

... a huge disappointment has been the loss of the yellow hammers ..
© Peter Partington 2006. www.peterpartington.fsnet.co.uk

For all intents and purposes then, everything appears to be much the same. But there are, no doubt, subtle differences, occasional signs which are indicating that, inexorably, some of the global changes that we now know are threatening us, are becoming apparent around here and, indeed, are already making their presence felt.

Helen, Olivia and I left West Penwith to come here to Weare Giffard. I worry about the rate of change in the environment that we shall all experience both locally, nationally and also worldwide within another eight years. Stephen, the young son on the nearby farm, will shortly be in his fifth year at junior school. Already, he accompanies his father as the latter 'shepherds' with his working dogs, which play a key role in helping the family cope with the yearly cycle of the flock of breeding ewes; indeed, it's fair bedlam around Netherdown Farm with the round-the-clock responsibilities during lambing time.

Will further changes occur during his senior school years? At any rate, during Year 6, I hope that he will have been made more aware of the problems facing creatures at the head of food chains than his predecessors; that awareness applies especially to those millions of youngsters who live in urban environments. We have failed, and are still failing, those youngsters. Remember over a decade ago and 'Education, Education, Education' as Tony Blair swept into Downing Street? In late June 2007, Gordon Brown succeeded Blair; his posturing has, naturally, been different, but the content of his rhetoric is varying only slightly and the end result is likely to be much the same as before. Too high a percentage of youngsters leave Year 6 each July still unaware of global warming. They are not acquainted with the reasons why it is happening, how and why it remains unchecked and how, therefore, its drastic increase over the past two decades continues. Most crucially, they are not being informed of its consequences for their future lives. The environment is now to be part of the senior school curriculum, announces Gordon Brown in July '07; but that's

Helen and Olivia, along with Shadow and Meggie, our young 'springer', join me to make the final corrections on the *Face to Face with Nature* manuscript.
© John Peacham, North Devon, 2007.

already too late, isn't it? There is no reason why the world's natural environments should not be an integral part of the National Curriculum at Key Stage 2. Imagine the amount of broad cross-curricular work that would be stimulated; more importantly though, how many eyes would be opened, at the same time, to the greatest challenge of our time.

Olivia has grown up with both domestic pets and tame individuals of some of our wild native animals and birds always close at hand. As a youngster, she accompanied Helen and I to those isolated places where we searched for our favourite creatures in their wild haunts. She grew to know the north Norfolk

This female cheetah was a close encounter with one of the 'Big Five', during my Game Ranger course on Shamwari Reserve, in the Eastern Cape of South Africa, in the summer of 2007.
© Olivia Chaffe

coast, west Wales and Cardiganshire and the Teifi valley in particular. Devon and Cornwall's north and south coasts have been the obvious first choice for most Bristolian families over decades for summer holidays; both Helen's and my family were no exception. As parents ourselves, we favoured West Penwith's remote Atlantic shoreline.

Olivia was rising five when Storm, the otter cub, was rescued by a postman on Exmoor. It was just before first light on a wet and cold February dawn in 1992 and the cub weighed just one pound seven ounces. Incredibly she survived, and Storm became a very close and integral part of our family life in north Somerset and a member of our unique family breeding group of British otters.

Subsequently, we lived for a time in, and then very close to, St Ives in Cornwall. There is no doubt that Olivia's love of the sea and all its associated wildlife, flourished from her time there. During all four seasons and whatever the weather, the cliff paths close to almost inaccessible and secretive beaches amidst the stunning scenery and wild nature of Cape Cornwall, Gurnards Head, Zennor and Wicca really do take some beating worldwide. D H Lawrence, once a Zennor resident, described the seas around the immediate headlands there as being 'peacock mingled'.

During the summer of 2006, Olivia joined a Frontier UK marine conservation expedition to Madagascar; a three and a half month long and unbelievably exciting journey studying the marine life of the Indian Ocean. Here she encountered turtles, manta rays, dolphins, sharks, dozens of fish species, corals and algae not to mention the lemurs in the forest zone. We have realised since her return that her list of species is endless. The experience of just being close to this whole new natural world will have been life forming. She concluded her journey by heading inland and living in a traditional village. There she taught English to young Malagasy children and shared her western European 'lifestyle' with families who have no electricity, no running water and where the lavatory is a place decided 'on the spur of the moment!'

Helen and I were delighted when Olivia decided to go to Madagascar. Her 'wildlife' experience was remarkable and will be unforgettable over a lifetime. Nevertheless, it was equally, if not more important, that Olivia should be aware of the circumstances under which most of humankind exists; that as one of the fortunate 'haves' living in the UK, she would become aware of the contribution she might make in the future to others who are less fortunate. However insignificant her input would appear at first, she would soon know by embracing the local lifestyles, customs and cultures, that apparently trivial acts of support, taken for granted by her upbringing, would make for real and meaningful improvement for others less fortunate. So we hoped that part of her time, too, in this still very remote island which is two and a half times the size of the UK, would be spent helping young people.

After reading Zoology at the University of Aberystwyth, we trust that Olivia, in her own inimitable way, will set about telling others that all is not well with Planet Earth. Will her degree course, and her encounters to date with whales, dolphins and other marine life which she has already experienced in Florida, Norway and Madagascar and most latterly her Southern African experience, persuade her to voice an important message? That message must be told here in the UK, as much as in any other of the developed nations in the world. That message? Quite simply, that we cannot go on taking from the world at the current rates, exploiting limited natural resources in order to satisfy our own apparently insatiable demands. All peoples, of all nations, should have equal access to, and an equal share of, the natural riches of this world.

The British government surely has enough influence to initiate reforms to the imbalance between the developed and less well-developed countries of the world. We ought to have the political leaders capable of leading in a way which takes into account the world's natural and wildlife resources. Then, we would belong to a nation that would be recognised for what it is doing positively for the future survival of the planet and humankind. At the present time, the UK is one of many nations that still puts itself first but continues to go through the motions in resolving major problems. Our government believes that its unending spin will convince people that it is taking positive and remedial action. Why does Bob Geldof need to question, within two years of the Edinburgh G8 summit, and this summer's conference at Heiligendamm in Germany, the degree of success achieved following the far-reaching promises made in a blaze of publicity by the United Kingdom and others? The truth is that in the past ten, maybe twenty years, the so-called highly developed and sophisticated UK has behaved little or no better and, sometimes, worse than other similar nations. To have lived, and to continue to live through this period of weakness and indecision has, frankly, been both disappointing and depressing.

It's now much later than I thought. The sun is setting fast and the evening light is fading. There's a chill in the air, typical of the shortening evenings. The mixed flock of swallows and house-martins which were so vociferous as they hawked for insects when I first arrived a couple of hours ago, are now in a long row on the telephone wires above me. One or two are busy preening but the rest are quite still as if in contemplation. Africa beckons; the swallows will spend Christmas and the New Year in South Africa, and the martins? No one knows exactly where they will travel, just somewhere south of the Sahara! I am looking forward to the day when we will know the answer. It is important to remember how little we still know about the natural world. Most Year 6 youngsters will be aware that man's past research and present technology allows the Challenger space shuttle to dock at the International

Space Station almost to the second. Yet are they aware of, or indeed are we even prepared to admit, the shortcomings in our knowledge of wild nature? Most of the birds now above me will have left within a month. I will come by one day as usual and all will be quiet; they will be on their way over Biscay, through the Atlas mountains of Morocco, before the hazardous trans-Saharan stage and eventually the Cape.

Families of robins and wrens, the loose 'clubs' of jackdaws and wagtails and several small flocks of chaffinches, goldfinches, green-

... Africa beckons, no one knows exactly where the martins will travel ...
© Peter Partington 2006. www.peterpartington.fsnet.co.uk

finches and linnets, along with the resident house sparrows will provide my close company, whenever I spend my daily time here during the next few months. However, emotionally, I acquire a real attachment every year to my summer friends, the swallows in particular. Yes, they do chatter away to me every summer evening; they are extraordinarily tame and trusting and I will experience a longing to see them again. In previous years, their first day back has inevitably been April 17th. This spring, Helen and I saw our frst swallows and sand martins over Halfpenny Bridge in Weare Giffard on the 4th. Is that another sign of a continuing trend over the past decade reflecting global warming of which we should be taking more notice, or did the birds simply second guess the overly warm weather which followed later in the month? The answer; it was the former, wasn't it? It was reported in the Independent, on June 19th 2007, that Arctic Bell heather has bloomed twenty days earlier this summer and that sanderling and dunlin had laid clutches an average of seven days earlier than a decade previously.

Meanwhile, next spring, I shall look out for the first swallows which will overnight in the same barn nearby and I shall be hoping to renew old acquaintances. Then, even on the very cold early spring days, they will gather what food they can over the same paddock. I used to have no doubt of witnessing their return but, nowadays, I wait with ever more apprehension.

Time now though for me to take a last glance for today along the water's edge. I haven't realised that the top of the tide must have passed a little while back, for the ebb is clearly running. Birds and fish, though, are still on the move and so, perhaps, is the local bitch otter. Have I missed something special with my mind focused elsewhere on the final details of this text? As I hear the different calls, so I can identify any new arrivals. However, the otter could have slipped past silently, and so, sadly, a rare opportunity would have gone unnoticed.

You know, all of our countryside is a wonderful resource, somewhere to retreat and recharge. That is certainly true for this place and like so many others I have experienced over the years.

To my regret the opportunities have either never arisen or were not grasped at the time, to experience blue whales amongst the sea ice of Antarctica, to marvel at condors spiralling to ever greater heights on thermals amongst the mountain peaks of the Andes, or to gaze at the still immeasurable herds of wild animals on their annual migration during the wet season in the Okavango, jewel of the Kalahari. Nevertheless, can you surpass the cacophony of sound and the spectacle of a hundred thousand pinkfooted geese on a winter dawn on the north Norfolk coast, or waited for a very long time with breath held and all conversation muted on the shore of a sea loch in the Western Isles? The reward? To hear, in dwindling light, the conversation between a bitch otter and her twin cubs fishing together as a family group in the kelp.

Nevertheless, I trust you are realising that *Face to face with nature* is not just about recalling experiences and dreaming about some of the wildlife wonders to be seen both in these islands and around the world. No, it is also about realising and understanding where our lifestyles are taking us, both as individuals and also as highly developed, industrialised nation states. Remember Neil Armstrong and fellow astronaut Edwin Aldrin on the *Apollo 11* mission; as Armstrong became the first person to touch the moon's surface he spoke the unforgettable phrase, "that's one small step for man, one giant leap for mankind." He and Aldrin explored for two and a half hours. Later, whilst communicating with Mission Control in Houston, Texas, he exclaimed,

"There's only one earth." Houston accepted his call.

However, Armstrong was back to them just moments later, and this time the sting was in the tail.

"And there's no spare one either," he added, from outer space.

Our futures must be built around sharing yet, at the same time, conserving with others, the limited resources of planet earth. What gives the United Kingdom the right more than any other nation, especially those we choose to criticise. Just remember some of our environmentalists constant clamouring against the United States of America, when having used our own natural resources by the 16th of April 2006, (ecological debt day), we then plunder our needs from the rest of the world for the remainder of that calendar year. In 1961 our ecological debt day was the 9th July; by 1981 it had moved forward to the 14th May. If annual global consumption levels matched those of the United Kingdom, it would take 3.1 Earths to meet our demands! The short and blunt answer to the question 'what right?' ... is 'none whatsoever'.

The recent and the present day actions and greed of most of the developed countries of the world mean that whatever corrective changes we instigate and put in place to reduce carbon emissions and our over-reliance on fossil fuels, will be ineffective. Even if we started in earnest tomorrow, we are still staring at a dramatic decline and deterioration in the quality of the world's diverse environments for at least the next twenty-five years. The challenge facing each one of us, *yes everyone of us*, is to *take* steps and not to talk about taking steps. If we cannot stop the growth of global warming, then surely we can greatly slow down the present annual rate of increase in levels of CO_2 emissions. Put simply, we have to 'walk our own talk' because we created the problem in the first place. We should now be leading the solutions.

Our present government has already announced that its targets for 2010 and beyond are more than likely to be missed; yet another promise hurriedly made, without any real interest in resolving the problem and without a true grip on the facts; in truth, the quality of the UK's present and future natural environments are being dismissed in yet another cloud of spin. The Kyoto Protocol expires in 2012 and must be re-negotiated and, this time, the USA, China, India and Brazil will have to be on board. There is already, therefore, a big question mark over whether the youngsters of today will be able to live lifestyles anywhere near approaching those we are currently enjoying and which we still take for granted; to be able to boast that we are making progress, by taking sensible and far-reaching actions, should mean that our youngsters and their children can look forward to living in varying environments worldwide, which will be safe, viable and thriving.

Every one of us can contribute because everyone is now aware of the problem, and there is no point in denying it, everyone is aware. You and I, along with our neighbours in the local community, must and really can, make a difference. Don't wait for the politicians who govern us to tell us what to do. They haven't done so to date. Why, because either they are gullible, more concerned about their mortgages or party to vested interests. Blair and Brown together, spun everything for ten years. So can Brown now be that different? Cameron thought that by flying the press corps to a Norweigian icefield he would prove he had solutions; Campbell's followers wait for him to decide the best way to jump, but by the time he does, it will be too late. All three and those they lead haven't much of a clue about the real environmental issues.

So make the changes yourself now, for yourself, and then for your family, please. Continue them again tomorrow and the day after that. It has to be every one of us, individually, who will make the difference.

A moment or two ago, I heard some very familiar and comforting sounds. No, it wasn't the whistle of an otter; if it had been, he or she would have been a distant relative of Storm, the remarkable creature who became so much part of our family life; Storm's wild grandmother gave birth to twin cubs upstream from Halspill Creek. Storm is buried here, close to the River Torridge. Way back in February 1992, it would have been inconceivable to think of that final scenario. Now, she will always be at rest alongside both Pebble and Ripple, two of my collection-bred bitches and with whom she spent most of her life, all three now so close to Storm's ancient family roots in the 'Land of the Two Rivers'.

No, the noise was the familiar piping from a family of redshanks, which as they arrived and claimed their preferred feeding place, disturbed some earlier arrivals, a curlew and a pair of oyster-catchers.

You will remember me recalling, at the very outset of the Face to Face story, that certain Saturday afternoon on the river Avon over fifty-five years ago now, and describing my excitement at identifying redshanks from my, then, only reference book, *The Observer's Book of Birds*.

Don't let us lose otters and redshanks from the estuaries of the Torridge and Avon; manta rays and dolphins from the coral reefs off Madagascar, or polar bears from the Greenland and Arctic ice-caps. If we do, our children's and their children's quality of life will be very poor; in fact, it could be too unacceptable to contemplate.

Are all of us prepared to come to terms with, and sooner rather than later, the depressing state of the world's environments? It is a beautiful life and an incredible world. Nevertheless, all of us are now quite aware, if they are not with us already, of the potential catastrophes which certainly lie just around the corner. Our excessive lifestyles are both practically and morally unjustifiable and wrong.

Our planet's long-term existence, our children's eventual survival and their future quality of life are of far greater importance.

I trust that you are enjoying *Face to Face with nature*, sharing some of my experiences from a journey of wonder which has been taking place for a long time now, a personal expedition arising from simple beginnings. If my luck holds, the odyssey has a good few more years yet to run. So I will continue, through my environmental and conservation lectures and writings to make people and particularly youngsters aware of the unparalleled beauty of our countryside and the problems we face.

Young people, still in their formative years at school, will face climate change and its inevitable consequences. Unless drastic measures are initiated now and, more importantly, are not just continually discussed, then those youngsters, by the time they are parents themselves, will be unable to find even partial resolutions to the difficulties.

We have been let down by a succession of politicians and a plethora of television naturalists who, without doubt, should have been fully aware of global warming, increased CO_2 emissions and world-wide famine for a long time now. Nevertheless, they have chosen, or have meekly accepted the advice of others, to stay silent.

You cannot call yourself a true naturalist unless you take into account the natural environment in which a particular species lives, when studying its status and its prospects of survival. I have referred fondly in earlier pages to iconic naturalists whose work gave me such

inspiration. Peter Scott, Ronald Lockley and Gerald Durrell studied their chosen subjects in their entirety, wildfowl, seabirds and lemurs respectively. Alive today, they would not have bowed to outside pressures; they would have spoken their minds; they would have persuaded others with their sound judgements. They would have taken into account not only their concern for the species but, also, for its immediate environment. As importantly though, they would have sought for a balance to

Olivia in the village of Antisikala in northern Madagascar. All peoples, of all nations, should have equal access to, and an equal share of, the natural riches of this world.
photograph © Rosie Butler 2006

be struck in any decision making by taking into account the needs of man himself. Finally, they would have asserted their strong moral convictions, arguing, for example, that our reliance on a fossil-fuel driven economy was, and still is, at best shortsighted and at worst, reprehensible, with regard to the future survival of Planet Earth.

By now reaffirming the severity of the situation, I entrust this message to each one of you, even to present-day naturalists, to be more truly committed. Nevertheless, I commend it most to those of you who are parents and to those of you who are in Year 6 and, therefore, in your final year in junior school. Embrace the message, sharing it with your parents and peers, as you embark on your journey to Further Education. I trust *Face to Face with nature* will convince you to think more conscientiously about that message and so to act more positively.

Yes, there are very many serious difficulties facing Planet Earth; no, they are not just going to go away and yes, governments, including our own, no matter by which administration they are controlled, have not to date, offered any cohesive or unbiased strategies. Don't be fooled or misled by what the partys' present leaders are currently saying about issues like energy shortfalls, with the question-marks of the nuclear and alternative energy options, CO_2 emissions and global warming. They spin the same evidence in different ways simply to earn your vote for their short-term political success. As with all politicians, vested interests will prevail and their every decision will be geared to speeding the further growth of the economy. The resources of the earth have become unrealistic to them and of no consequence; nevertheless, in their eyes the financial returns must be immediately tangible.

speckled woods ... seemingly endlessly chasing one another
© Peter Partington 2006. www.peterpartington.fsnet.co.uk

As you close this book, pause, take some time out and then make some personal and family changes. You could set up water butts from existing downpipes, put 'hippos' in toilet systems, switch off the stand-by for televisions, videos and dvds, and fit your household with energy-saving lightbulbs, (if every household replaced just three ordinary light bulbs, the energy saved would provide all the energy for Britain's street lights); you could compile green compost and not buy the 4X4 to cruise the urban roads; it should be a necessity not a fashion accessory! None of these are drastic, or life-changing decisions, but could be significant to you and your family's way of living. In turn though, it will affect your local community, the environment in your workplace and your school; ... it's all about not cheating on the next generation! ...

It will be a spiritual matter of how we see ourselves as members of both local and larger communities, but it's the only way to ring the changes, to begin the significant reversal of events which we have conveniently ignored for so long.

Each one of you, every individual, can, should, and I believe will want to, make his or her own further personal choices and contributions. Maybe, you will feel it is too late to reduce climatic change significantly and so make long-lasting impacts on the environment. Nevertheless, it is not too late to tackle the issues and to confront the major challenge of the second and third decades of the 21st century.

We are wrecking nature, of that there is no doubt; the planet is utterly different now. The ever higher carbon dioxide levels are causing rising sea-levels; we have been creating and accelerating the greenhouse effect, not just last year but for some time. We are going to have to live on a planet where, in some places already, nature is no longer nature. What is already clear is that we are heading for a temperature rise of at least 2 degrees centigrade which over time will melt the Greenland glaciers. Is the end of nature, as we recognise it now, possibly in sight?

There have been many who suspected and feared this ecological holocaust; a few were in the position to influence government policy; nevertheless, as I have written, many of those individuals, some of whom you would classify as 'household name' naturalists, or bodies that were committed to the conservation cause, have been singularly reticent for reasons only known to themselves. So, man's actions have left nature irredeemably altered.

Even, accepting all that, we should still be dissatisfied and disappointed with ourselves. For really, we are the problem; we should be responding to our own guilt and to our own deceit. Any chance of slowing down the inexorable processes does not lie with governments, but perhaps after all, with you and me. We want legislation, we want, we are waiting for, politicians to tell us what to do, to legislate or, simply, to do something for us. We have a duty to slow the processes which we have been measuring and whose consequences we have been observing; we have a duty to give future generations a greater chance of survival.

However, we have not been prepared to do much for ourselves. That's up to now. Now we face no alternative. We should be telling young people of the fantastic opportunities which are there to be grasped, to realise what is most important in life and to correct the mistakes previous generations have made and that we continue to make.

In 'An Inconvenient Truth', Al Gore's 2006 film on climate change, he explains part of the problem. "It is difficult to get a man to understand something when his salary depends upon him not understanding it." But, also in 2006, Jim Hansen commented, "We have a very brief window to deal with climate change ... no longer than a decade at most."

That's our dilemma; nevertheless, the truth, my friends, is that there is little that matters more than the future of the planet itself.

I wanted my Wildlife Park, from its conception in the early '60s, to be much more than a comprehensive collection of native animals and birds.

From my early associations with Peter Scott and Ronald Lockley, I had already realised that I needed to speak about the fast emerging threats to our native wildlife to a wider audience. I admit that, at first, I was entirely concerned with the problems facing certain species. I would respond to a pressing issue of the day; for example, the threat to our seabirds caused by repeated spillages of oil. This was highlighted by the grounding of the Torrey Canyon off the coast of west Cornwall in 1967.

On all my literature were the words **'Conservation through Education'**, indeed, that was also the title of my early lectures. The quote with which I would conclude was: **"The wildlife of today is not ours to dispose of as we please; we have it in trust; we must account for it to those who come after."** King George VI.

Some years later, I had acquired Joseph Cornell's book *Sharing Nature with Children*. Cornell wrote in the spirit of Rachel Carson; she said that when you introduced youngsters to the excitement of the natural world that **"it is not half so important to *know* as to *feel*."** So, the content of my talks continued to evolve and by now, in the '80s, I was finishing my presentations with Cornell's words:

"In today's world of overpopulation and high consumption, it is essential that we keep youngsters in touch with the earth; its changing seasons, its natural rhythms, its beauty and its mysteries; in fact, nothing will suffice short of teaching youngsters to love nature ... and to love life."

Nevertheless, I have again moved on. Today, as I close with my audiences, I refer to the words of Gerald Durrell, the third influential member of the Scott, Lockley and Durrell triumvirate:

"The world is as delicate and as complicated as a spider's web. If you touch one thread, you send shivers running through all the other threads; however we're not just touching the web, we're tearing great holes in it."

For the foreseeable future I will still finish with Durrell's words. However nowadays, I commence my lectures, which are nearly always illustrated with Phantom, my daughter Olivia's tame barn owl, with a brief but sobering factual resumé. It allows me to summarise how my thoughts have, and still are continuing to evolve over forty years; that we must realise, as never before, how man's eventual survival will only be secured by understanding that we are not separate from, or divorced from, the natural world.

Now my opening words always are:

"If the world were a village, imagine 100 people live in that village; 9 would speak English, 24 would have television sets, 17 would be unable to read, but 60, yes 60, would be hungry." David J Smith, Shelagh Armstrong.

That really does put matters into perspective, doesn't it!

Over the past three years I have increasingly found individuals and companies who have been prepared to contribute copies of *Stormforce, an otter's tale* as a literary resource for the Year 6 classes of their local Community Junior Schools. Nearly 100 schools have been supported by

benefactors and my innovative idea has been featured on the BBC Countryfile programme. It is clear that *Stormforce* has been widely welcomed as it finds it place in those schools which are concerned to educate and not merely to instruct.

I will continue to find sponsors for *Stormforce* which *Face to Face* will now complement. I also regularly speak to other audiences, young and old alike; for further information please telephone, write or email; the details you require are elsewhere in *Face to Face*. I shall look forward to hearing from you.

First steps ... David Chaffe introduces youngsters to a barn owl, and so to the evolution, beauty and mysteries of nature.